The Analects of Confucius

A Selection of the Sayings of Mencius

The Way and Its Power of Laozi

The Analects of Confucius
A Selection of the Sayings of Mencius
The Way and Its Power of Laozi

English Translation
by James Legge

Preface
by John S. Bowman

Signature Press
EDITIONS

Published by World Publications Group, Inc.
140 Laurel Street
East Bridgewater, MA 02333
www.wrldpub.net

The present text of *The Analects of Confucius*, *A Selection of the Sayings of Mencius*, and *The Way and Its Power of Laozi* derive from James Legge's editions.

Published in 2008 by World Publications Group, Inc., with new preface.

ISBN 978-1-57215-288-5
ISBN 1-57215-288-5
Printed and bound in China by SNP Leefung Printers Limited.

1 2 3 4 5 06 05 03 02

CONTENTS

PREFACE

For many years now, an unusual historical phenomenon has been noted: from the sixth through the fourth centuries B.C.—that is, between about 600 and 300 B.C.—an extraordinary group of individuals appeared in several cultures around the world, individuals who dealt with the most fundamental and universal issues of life. Why this occurred, whether it was mere coincidence or reflected a certain state of being that *Homo sapiens* attained during this period of time, is a subject for debate. In any case, these individuals or their disciples recorded their thoughts in works that continue to this day to be among the most profound and influential books ever written.

In India, for instance, Siddartha Gautama, who would become known as the Buddha ("the awakened one"), lived and taught during this period. (His birth is variously dated from 623 to 445 B.C., his death from 543 to 365 B.C.) It is also the time of Vardhamana Mahavira, the founder of Jainism, an offshoot of Hinduism and Buddhism. For the Jews, this was the time of the prophet Jeremiah, and although it is not possible to pin these books down to individuals, it is during this period that the Torah, the first five books of the Old Testament, were written by the Hebrews. It was also the time when many of the sacred texts of Hinduism were recorded—including the *Bhagavad Gita*. In Greece, this was the period of the great philosophers: Thales, Heraclitus, and Parmenides are perhaps not that well known today, but Pythagoras (?580 B.C.–?), Socrates (?469–399 B.C.), Plato (?427–?327 B.C.), and Aristotle (?445–?385 B.C.) certainly are.

The subject of this book is the thinking of three Chinese philosophers of this period: K'ung-fu-tzu (or Kongfuzi) (?551–479 B.C.), known to the West as Confucius; Men Gzi (?372–?279 B.C.), known to the West as Mencius; and Laozi (or LaoTse) (sixth century B.C.). They have much in common. Many details about the lives of the three are questioned by some scholars—even whether there ever lived individuals by these names or whether the texts attributed to them were actually written by others. (If this seems a bit unsettling, consider that many scholars question whether there ever was an individual named Homer who wrote the Greek epic poems.) Their birth and death dates vary greatly depending on certain traditions; the fundamental texts attributed to them were almost certainly not set down by the masters themselves but by disciples; although none of these individuals propounded a religious faith or system, their texts have assumed an almost sacred status in their own cultures and followers have in some instances established religious sects based on them; and finally, all three have long enjoyed an honored status in the West, their works continually translated and widely read, and in the case of one—Laozi—even enjoying almost cult status.[1]

---

1. It should be noted that the English translations of their works are often assigned different titles. Readers will also note that there is some inconsistency in the spelling of Chinese names and other words, both within in this volume and compared to those in other books. This is due to the different systems of transliterating Chinese—in turn, based on the closest approximation to the Chinese sounds. The modern system, for instance, prefers Laozi to Lao Tse, and Dao instead of Tao. The translations provided here are those of James Legge, the Scottish Christian missionary to China and later Oxford scholar whose translations were responsible for making so many of the classic Chinese texts known to the English-speaking world; because they date from the mid-19th century they employ many spellings no longer in use. None of this, however, affects the essential significance of the texts.

Confucius and his *Analects* are arguably the most influential of the three. One scholar has asserted, "No other book in the entire history of the world has exerted a greater influence on a larger number or people over a longer period of time than this slim volume."

The Analects is basically a collection of aphorisms, or maxims—relatively terse statements offering insights and advice. "Analects," in fact, means nothing more than "selected sayings" and remains the English title of this work because an early translator settled on it. Underlying these maxims is the goal of pursuing such virtues as filial piety and obedience, seeking moderation and harmony, engaging in personal education and culture, and striving for social order and peace. Taken as a whole, *The Analects* is an ethical doctrine, not a religious one, even though many of its precepts echo various religions' teachings. If it were to be listed on a modern bestsellers list, it would fall somewhere between the self-improvement books and guides to better leadership, but unlike today's counterparts, *The Analects* is as much concerned with society's well-being as with that of the individual.

The name "Confucius" is the Latinized transliteration (by seventeenth century Jesuits) of how he came to be known in China, K'ung-fu-tzu, which means "Great Master Kung." There is little factual evidence on which to reconstruct his life, but all standard accounts tend to fix his birth year at 551 B.C. and his death year at 479 B.C. His father is said to have been a minor aristocrat, but both parents died when he was quite young and he grew up in poverty. Although he would gain appointment to some minor offices, he failed in his efforts to attain a high government office, where he could be in a position to reform society according to his precepts. He seems to have been a teacher, and as such he attracted a group of followers or disciples, sometimes specified as 3,000, sometimes as 72, but like so much about his life either figure is probably legendary.

If Confucius ever wrote a book, it was not published in his lifetime. Instead, his teachings allegedly were recorded by his students and followers. In any case, *The Analects* so widely read today is a compilation of chapters, or books, dating from different periods and from different sources—some of these not particularly consistent with Confucius' philosophy. Some scholars even question whether much of the text ever originated with Confucius. Several versions of *The Analects* were known in the centuries following his death, but by about A.D. 175 the Chinese government had an approved version that was virtually the same as the one known today. In the twelfth century a Chinese scholar, Zhu Xi, selected what is known as the *Four Books*, the four essential texts of Confucianism, with the *Analects* as its core; these books and Zhu Xi's commentaries on them would become the basis for China's civil service examinations in the following centuries.

From that point on, Confucianism became, in effect, the official creed of China. Although it was never a religion, temples are dedicated to Confucius. Confucianism also was adopted in many countries, especially Korea, Japan, and Vietnam, but nowhere else did it assume the role it did in China, where it served not only as a guide to the individual's moral life and responsibilities but also as the underlying philosophy of society and the state.

Long before Confucianism was formally adopted by Chinese governments, indeed almost immediately after Confucius himself died, his philosophy was being expounded and expanded upon by other Chinese sages. Chief among these early promoters of Confucianism was Men Gzi, or Mencius. He was born about 370 B.C. and is said to have studied philosophy with the grandson of Confucius. Like Confucius he traveled about, teaching and trying to persuade the various, often warring, provincial leaders to adopt his philosophy. But Mencius went beyond Confucius and claimed that the people had a right to revolt against a ruler who did not govern with justice, morality, and regard to his people's well-being. He also stressed the role of education in creating a society where citizens could attain their full potential. Above all, Mencius stressed that human nature is fundamentally good.

Mencius had little success in his lifetime, and it was only thanks to some of his followers that his ideas were set down in a series of dialogues, a work known as *The Mencius* (but which we here title *A Selection of the Sayings of Mencius*). Even then his ideas were ignored until the twelfth century, when, as noted above, the scholar Zhu Xi assembled the essential texts of Confucianism in the *Four Books* and chose to include the work attributed to Mencius. Because the Chinese original of *The Mencius* is so long, we provide only the opening section, but it gives a good sense of both the tenor and flavor of this work.

There is little solid evidence for the details of the lives of Confucius and Mencius, but even less is known about the life of the third of our wise men, Laozi. Tradition claims that he was a slightly older contemporary of Confucius and even that the two met at least once. Several other traditions make him seem virtually a mythical being. Even those who accept that there was an individual by this name are willing to accept that the work attributed to him, the *Dao De Jing* (*The Way and Its Power*) was not written until two or three centuries after his death and that it is most likely the work of several scholars.

The philosophical system laid out in this work is known as Daoism, or Taoism, and in some respects it is the opposite of

Confucianism but in other respects it complements it. Where Confucianism is prescriptive and practical, communal and activist, Daoism is liberating and transcendental, individualistic and passive. On the other hand, individuals—including the rulers of China—are encouraged to follow "the Way" (*dao*) in order to achieve many of the same goals advocated by Confucianism: moderation, harmony, peace. However, because the *Dao de Jing* is often vague and is rife with paradoxes and witty sayings, people have been able to read just about anything they want into it.

In the course of China's long history since these three Masters and their works appeared on the scene, their writings and ideas, their followers and institutions have not always had a perfectly easy time. There were many schools of Confucianism, for instance, and often they competed against one another. Daoism in particular took new forms: at one point in the late second century A.D., some of its followers made it into a religion stressing the confession of sins, performing good deeds, and the promise of immortality; in this form, Laozi himself became deified as a messiah of the Great Peace. There were constant struggles among adherents to Confucianism and Daoism and Buddhism to retain the support of China's masses as well as its rulers. Even in the twentieth century, the Communist dictator Mao Zedong is said to have been influenced by both Confucius and Laozi, although Confucianism was attacked as promoting a society governed by an elite (and what Mao did with their teachings is a far cry from either Master's philosophy).

In the Western world, these three works have met various fates. *The Sayings of Mencius* is the least known of the works. *The Analects* has received numerous translations, and the maxims of Confucius, both actual ones and many falsely attributed to him, are often cited. The words of Laozi have had the most unexpected fate. In recent decades, the concept of Dao (often spelled as Tao) — "the Way," "The Path"—has been adopted by various disciplines and belief systems as meaning the most natural and appropriate way to attain the goal sought. Thus we have books such as *The Tao of Physics*, *The Tao of Pooh* (yes, Winnie-the-Pooh), *The Tao of Leadership*, *The Tao of Health, Sex and Longevity*. We have Wayne Dyer, a popular inspirational speaker, offering *Change Your Thoughts—Change your Life: The Wisdom of the Tao*. And then there are the websites such as "The Tao of Programming," "The Tao of Mac," "The Tao of Backup."

Clearly, Daoism has taken a path not foreseen by Laozi: a New Age fad. But readers can see just what it is about these three texts that have made them the classics of Chinese culture. All three are quite transparent as philosophical writings go, and although all have elements that will seem somewhat foreign and exotic to Western readers, they still have much relevance to our own lives and times.

John S. Bowman

The Analects of
Confucius

Book I

HSIO R

CHAPTER I. 1. The Master said, "Is it not pleasant to learn with a constant perseverance and application?

2. "Is it not delightful to have friends coming from distant quarters?

3. "Is he not a man of complete virtue who feels no discomposure though men may take no note of him?"

CHAPTER II. 1. The philosopher Yu said, "They are few who, being filial and fraternal, are fond of offending against their superiors. There have been none who, not liking to offend against their superiors, have been fond of stirring up confusion.

2. "The superior man bends his attention to what is radical.

That being established, all practical courses naturally grow up. Filial piety and fraternal submission! Are they not the root of all benevolent actions?"

CHAPTER III. The Master said, "Fine words and an insinuating appearance are seldom associated with true virtue."

CHAPTER IV. The philosopher Tsang said, "I daily examine myself on three points: whether, in transacting business for others, I may have been not faithful; whether, in intercourse with friends, I may have been not sincere; whether I may have not mastered and practised the instructions of my teacher."

CHAPTER V. The Master said, "To rule a country of a thousand chariots, there must be reverent attention to business, and sincerity; economy in expenditure, and love for men; and the employment of the people at the proper seasons."

CHAPTER VI. The Master said, "A youth, when at home, should be filial, and, abroad, respectful to his elders. He should be earnest and truthful. He should overflow in love to all, and cultivate the friendship of the good. When he has time and opportunity, after the performance of these things, he should employ them in polite studies."

CHAPTER VII. Tsze-hsia said, "If a man withdraws his mind from the love of beauty, and applies it as sincerely to the love of the virtuous; if, in serving his parents, he can exert his utmost strength; if, in serving his prince, he can devote his life; if, in his intercourse with his friends, his words are sincere: although men say that he has not learned, I will certainly say that he has."

CHAPTER VIII. 1. The Master said, "If the scholar be not grave, he will not call forth any veneration, and his learning will not be solid.

2. "Hold faithfulness and sincerity as first principles.

3. "Have no friends not equal to yourself.

4. "When you have faults, do not fear to abandon them."

CHAPTER IX. The philosopher Tsang said, "Let there be a careful attention to perform the funeral rites to parents, and let them be followed when long gone with the ceremonies of sacrifice; then the virtue of the people will resume its proper excellence."

CHAPTER X. 1. Tsze-ch'in asked Tsze-kung, saying, "When our Master comes to any country, he does not fail to learn all about its government. Does he ask his information? Or is it given to him?"

2. Tsze-kung said, "Our Master is benign, upright, courteous, temperate, and complaisant, and thus he gets his information. The Master's mode of asking information! Is it not different from that of other men?"

CHAPTER XI. The Master said, "While a man's father is alive, look at the bent of his will; when his father is dead, look at his conduct. If for three years he does not alter from the way of his father, he may be called filial."

CHAPTER XII. 1. The philosopher Yu said, "In practising the rules of propriety, a natural ease is to be prized. In the ways prescribed by the ancient kings, this is the excellent quality, and in things small and great we follow them.

2. "Yet it is not to be observed in all cases. If one, knowing how such ease should be prized, manifests it, without regulating it by the rules of propriety, this likewise is not to be done."

CHAPTER XIII. The philosopher Yu said, "When agreements are made according to what is right, what is spoken can be made good. When respect is shown according to what is proper, one keeps far from shame and disgrace. When the parties upon whom a man leans are proper persons to be intimate with, he can make them his guides and masters."

CHAPTER XIV. The Master said, "He who aims to be a man of complete virtue in his food does not seek to gratify his appetite, nor in his dwelling place does he seek the appliances of ease; he is earnest in what he is doing, and careful in his speech; he frequents the company of men of principle that he may be rectified: such a person may be said indeed to love to learn."

CHAPTER XV. 1. Tsze-kung said, "What do you pronounce concerning the poor man who yet does not flatter, and the rich man who is not proud?" The Master replied, "They will do; but they are not equal to him who, though poor, is yet cheerful, and to him who, though rich, loves the rules of propriety."

2. Tsze-kung replied, "It is said in the 'Book of Poetry,' 'As you cut and then file, as you carve and then polish.' The meaning is the same, I apprehend, as that which you have just expressed."

3. The Master said, "With one like Ts'ze, I can begin to talk about the odes. I told him one point, and he knew its proper sequence."

CHAPTER XVI. The Master said, "I will not be afflicted at men's not knowing me; I will be afflicted that I do not know men."

Book II

WEI CHANG

CHAPTER I. The Master said, "He who exercises government by means of his virtue may be compared to the north polar star, which keeps its place and all the stars turn towards it."

CHAPTER II. The Master said, "In the 'Book of Poetry' are three hundred pieces, but the design of them all may be embraced in one sentence 'Having no depraved thoughts.' "

CHAPTER III. 1. The Master said, "If the people be led by laws, and uniformity sought to be given them by punishments, they will try to avoid the punishment, but have no sense of shame.

2. "If they be led by virtue, and uniformity sought to be given them by the rules of propriety, they will have the sense of shame, and moreover will become good."

CHAPTER IV. 1. The Master said, "At fifteen, I had my mind bent on learning.

2. "At thirty, I stood firm."

3. "At forty, I had no doubts."

4. "At fifty, I knew the decrees of Heaven."

5. "At sixty, my ear was an obedient organ for the reception of truth."

6. "At seventy, I could follow what my heart desired, without transgressing what was right."

CHAPTER V. 1. Mang I asked what filial piety was. The Master said, "It is not being disobedient."

2. Soon after, as Fan Ch'ih was driving him, the Master told him, saying, "Mang-sun asked me what filial piety was, and I answered him, 'Not being disobedient.' "

3. Fan Ch'ih said, "What did you mean?" The Master replied, "That parents, when alive, be served according to propriety; that, when dead, they should be buried according to propriety; and that they should be sacrificed to according to propriety."

CHAPTER VI. Mang Wu asked what filial piety was. The Master said, "Parents are anxious lest their children should be sick."

CHAPTER VII. Tsze-yu asked what filial piety was. The Master said, "The filial piety of nowadays means the support of one's parents. But dogs and horses likewise are able to do something in the way of support; without reverence, what is there to distinguish the one support given from the other?"

CHAPTER VIII. Tsze-hsia asked what filial piety was. The Master said, "The difficulty is with the countenance. If, when their elders have any troublesome affairs, the young take the toil of them, and if, when the young have wine and food, they set them before their elders, is THIS to be considered filial piety?"

CHAPTER IX. The Master said, "I have talked with Hui for a whole day, and he has not made any objection to anything I said—as if he were stupid. He has retired, and I have examined his conduct when away from me, and found him able to illustrate my teachings. Hui! He is not stupid."

CHAPTER X. 1. The Master said, "See what a man does.

2. "Mark his motives.

3. "Examine in what things he rests.

4. "How can a man conceal his character?"

CHAPTER XI. The Master said, "If a man keeps cherishing his old knowledge, so as continually to be acquiring new, he may be a teacher of others."

CHAPTER XII. The Master said, "The accomplished scholar is not a utensil."

CHAPTER XIII. Tsze-kung asked what constituted the superior man. The Master said, "He acts before he speaks, and afterwards speaks according to his actions."

CHAPTER XIV. The Master said, "The superior man is catholic and not partisan. The mean man is partisan and not catholic."

CHAPTER XV. The Master said, "Learning without thought is labour lost; thought without learning is perilous."

CHAPTER XVI. The Master said, "The study of strange doctrines is injurious indeed!"

CHAPTER XVII. The Master said, "Yu, shall I teach you what knowledge is? When you know a thing, to hold that you know it; and when you do not know a thing, to allow that you do not know it—this is knowledge."

CHAPTER XVIII. 1. Tsze-chang was learning with a view to official emolument.

2. The Master said, "Hear much and put aside the points of which you stand in doubt, while you speak cautiously at the same time of the others: then you will afford few occasions for blame. See much and put aside the things which seem perilous, while you are cautious at the same time in carrying the others into practice: then you will have few occasions for repentance. When one gives few occasions for blame in his words, and few occasions for repentance in his conduct, he is in the way to get emolument."

CHAPTER XIX. The Duke Ai asked, saying, "What should be done in order to secure the submission of the people?" Confucius replied, "Advance the upright and set aside the crooked, then the people will submit. Advance the crooked and set aside the upright, then the people will not submit."

CHAPTER XX. Chi K'ang asked how to cause the people to reverence their ruler, to be faithful to him, and to go on to nerve themselves to virtue. The Master said, "Let him preside over them with gravity; then they will reverence him. Let him be filial and kind to all; then they will be faithful to him. Let him advance the good and teach the incompetent; then they will eagerly seek to be virtuous."

CHAPTER XXI. 1. Someone addressed Confucius, saying, "Sir, why are you not engaged in the government?"

2. The Master said, "What does the Shu-ching say of filial piety? 'You are filial, you discharge your brotherly duties. These qualities are displayed in government.' This then also constitutes the exercise of government. Why must there be THAT—making one be in the government?"

CHAPTER XXII. The Master said, "I do not know how a man without truthfulness is to get on. How can a large carriage be made to go without the crossbar for yoking the oxen to, or a small carriage without the arrangement for yoking the horses?"

CHAPTER XXIII. 1. Tsze-chang asked whether the affairs of ten ages after could be known.

2. Confucius said, "The Yin dynasty followed the regulations of the Hsia: wherein it took from or added to them may be known. The Chau dynasty has followed the regulations of Yin: wherein it took from or added to them may be known. Some other may follow the Chau, but though it should be at the distance of a hundred ages, its affairs may be known."

CHAPTER XXIV. 1. The Master said, "For a man to sacrifice to a spirit which does not belong to him is flattery.

2. "To see what is right and not to do it is want of courage."

Book III

PA YIH

CHAPTER I. Confucius said of the head of the Chi family, who had eight rows of pantomimes in his area, "If he can bear to do this, what may he not bear to do?"

CHAPTER II. The three families used the YUNG ode, while the vessels were being removed, at the conclusion of the sacrifice. The Master said, " 'Assisting are the princes: the son of Heaven looks profound and grave': what application can these words have in the hall of the three families?"

CHAPTER III. The Master said, "If a man be without the virtues proper to humanity, what has he to do with the rites of propriety? If a man be without the virtues proper to humanity, what has he to do with music?"

CHAPTER IV. 1. Lin Fang asked what was the first thing to be attended to in ceremonies.

2. The Master said, "A great question indeed!

3. "In festive ceremonies, it is better to be sparing than extravagant.

In the ceremonies of mourning, it is better that there be deep sorrow than a minute attention to observances."

CHAPTER V. The Master said, "The rude tribes of the east and north have their princes, and are not like the States of our great land which are without them."

CHAPTER VI. The chief of the Chi family was about to sacrifice to the T'ai mountain. The Master said to Zan Yu, "Can you not save him from this?" He answered, "I cannot." Confucius said, "Alas! will you say that the T'ai mountain is not so discerning as Lin Fang?"

CHAPTER VII. The Master said, "The student of virtue has no contentions. If it be said he cannot avoid them, shall this be in archery? But he bows complaisantly to his competitors; thus he ascends the hall, descends, and exacts the forfeit of drinking. In his contention, he is still the Chun-tsze."

CHAPTER VIII. 1. Tsze-hsia asked, saying, "What is the meaning of the passage 'The pretty dimples of her artful smile! The well-defined black and white of her eye! The plain ground for the colours'?"

2. The Master said, "The business of laying on the colours follows the preparation of the plain ground."

3. "Ceremonies then are a subsequent thing?" The Master said, "It is Shang who can bring out my meaning. Now I can begin to talk about the odes with him."

CHAPTER IX. The Master said, "I could describe the ceremonies of the Hsia dynasty, but Chi cannot sufficiently attest my words. I could describe the ceremonies of the Yin dynasty, but Sung cannot sufficiently attest my words. They cannot do so because of the insufficiency of their records and wise men. If those were sufficient, I could adduce them in support of my words."

CHAPTER X. The Master said, "At the great sacrifice, after the pouring out of the libation, I have no wish to look on."

CHAPTER XI. Someone asked the meaning of the great sacrifice. The Master said, "I do not know. He who knew its meaning would find it as easy to govern the kingdom as to look on this"—pointing to his palm.

CHAPTER XII. 1. He sacrificed to the dead, as if they were present. He sacrificed to the spirits, as if the spirits were present.

2. The Master said, "I consider my not being present at the sacrifice as if I did not sacrifice."

CHAPTER XIII. 1. Wang-sun Chia asked, saying, "What is the meaning of the saying 'It is better to pay court to the furnace than to the southwest corner'?"

2. The Master said, "Not so. He who offends against Heaven has none to whom he can pray."

CHAPTER XIV. The Master said, "Chau had the advantage of viewing the two past dynasties. How complete and elegant are its regulations! I follow Chau."

CHAPTER XV. The Master, when he entered the grand temple, asked about everything. Someone said, "Who will say that the son of the man of Tsau knows the rules of propriety! He has entered the grand temple and asks about everything." The Master heard the remark and said, "This is a rule of propriety."

CHAPTER XVI. The Master said, "In archery it is not going through the leather which is the principal thing—because people's strength is not equal. This was the old way."

CHAPTER XVII. 1. Tsze-kung wished to do away with the offering of a sheep connected with the inauguration of the first day of each month.

2. The Master said, "Ts'ze, you love the sheep; I love the ceremony."

CHAPTER XVIII. The Master said, "The full observance of the rules of propriety in serving one's prince is accounted by people to be flattery."

CHAPTER XIX. The Duke Ting asked how a prince should employ his ministers, and how ministers should serve their prince. Confucius replied, "A prince should employ his minister according to the rules of propriety; ministers should serve their prince with faithfulness."

CHAPTER XX. The Master said, "The Kwan Tsu is expressive of enjoyment without being licentious, and of grief without being hurtfully excessive."

CHAPTER XXI. 1. The Duke Ai asked Tsai Wo about the altars of the spirits of the land. Tsai Wo replied, "The Hsia sovereign planted the pine tree about them; the men of the Yin planted the cypress; and the men of the Chau planted the chestnut tree, meaning thereby to cause the people to be in awe."

2. When the Master heard it, he said, "Things that are done, it is needless to speak about; things that have had their course, it is needless to remonstrate about; things that are past, it is needless to blame."

CHAPTER XXII. 1. The Master said, "Small indeed was the capacity of Kwan Chung!"

2. Someone said, "Was Kwan Chung parsimonious?" "Kwan," was the reply, "had the San Kwei, and his officers performed no double duties; how can he be considered parsimonious?"

3. "Then, did Kwan Chung know the rules of propriety?" The Master said, "The princes of States have a screen intercepting the view at their gates. Kwan had likewise a screen at his gate. The princes of States, on any friendly meeting between two of them, had a stand on which to place their inverted cups. Kwan had also such a stand. If Kwan knew the rules of propriety, who does not know them?"

CHAPTER XXXII. The Master instructing the grand music-master of Lu said, "How to play music may be known. At the commencement of the piece, all the parts should sound together. As it proceeds, they should be in harmony while severally distinct and flowing without break, and thus on to the conclusion."

CHAPTER XXIV. The border warden at Yi requested to be introduced to the Master, saying, "When men of superior virtue have come to this, I have never been denied the privilege of seeing them." The followers of the sage introduced him, and when he came out from the interview, he said, "My friends, why are you distressed by your master's loss of office? The kingdom has long been without the principles of truth and right; Heaven is going to use your master as a bell with its wooden tongue."

CHAPTER XXV. The Master said of the Shao that it was perfectly beautiful and also perfectly good. He said of the Wu that it was perfectly beautiful but not perfectly good.

CHAPTER XXVI. The Master said, "High station filled without indulgent generosity; ceremonies performed without reverence; mourning conducted without sorrow—wherewith should I contemplate such ways?"

Book IV

LE JIN

CHAPTER I. The Master said, "It is virtuous manners which constitute the excellence of a neighborhood. If a man in selecting a residence do not fix on one where such prevail, how can he be wise?"

CHAPTER II. The Master said, "Those who are without virtue cannot abide long either in a condition of poverty and hardship, or in a condition of enjoyment. The virtuous rest in virtue; the wise desire virtue."

CHAPTER III. The Master said, "It is only the truly virtuous man who can love, or who can hate, others."

CHAPTER IV. The Master said, "If the will be set on virtue, there will be no practice of wickedness."

CHAPTER V. 1. The Master said, "Riches and honours are what men desire. If it cannot be obtained in the proper way, they should not be held. Poverty and meanness are what men dislike. If it cannot be avoided in the proper way, they should not be avoided.

2. "If a superior man abandon virtue, how can he fulfil the requirements of that name?

3. "The superior man does not, even for the space of a single meal, act contrary to virtue. In moments of haste, he cleaves to it. In seasons of danger, he cleaves to it."

CHAPTER VI. 1. The Master said, "I have not seen a person who loved virtue, or one who hated what was not virtuous. He who loved virtue would esteem nothing above it. He who hated what is not virtuous would practise virtue in such a way that he would not allow anything that is not virtuous to approach his person.

2. "Is anyone able for one day to apply his strength to virtue? I have not seen the case in which his strength would be insufficient.

3. "Should there possibly be any such case, I have not seen it."

CHAPTER VII. The Master said, "The faults of men are characteristic of the class to which they belong. By observing a man's faults, it may be known that he is virtuous."

CHAPTER VIII. The Master said, "If a man in the morning hear the right way, he may die in the evening without regret."

CHAPTER IX. The Master said, "A scholar, whose mind is set on truth, and who is ashamed of bad clothes and bad food, is not fit to be discoursed with."

CHAPTER X. The Master said, "The superior man, in the world, does not set his mind either for anything, or against anything; what is right he will follow."

CHAPTER XI. The Master said, "The superior man thinks of virtue; the small man thinks of comfort. The superior man thinks of the sanctions of law; the small man thinks of favours which he may receive."

CHAPTER XII. The Master said: "He who acts with a constant view to his own advantage will be much murmured against."

CHAPTER XIII. The Master said, "If a prince is able to govern his kingdom with the complaisance proper to the rules of propriety, what difficulty will he have? If he cannot govern it with that complaisance, what has he to do with the rules of propriety?"

CHAPTER XIV. The Master said, "A man should say, I am not concerned that I have no place, I am concerned how I may fit myself for one. I am not concerned that I am not known, I seek to be worthy to be known."

CHAPTER XV. 1. The Master said, "Shan, my doctrine is that of an all-pervading unity." The disciple Tsang replied, "Yes."

2. The Master went out, and the other disciples asked, saying, "What do his words mean?" Tsang said, "The doctrine of our Master is to be true to the principles of our nature and the benevolent exercise of them to others—this and nothing more."

CHAPTER XVI. The Master said, "The mind of the superior man is conversant with righteousness; the mind of the mean man is conversant with gain."

CHAPTER XVII. The Master said, "When we see men of worth, we should think of equalling them; when we see men of a contrary character, we should turn inwards and examine ourselves."

CHAPTER XVIII. The Master said, "In serving his parents, a son may remonstrate with them, but gently; when he sees that they do not incline to follow his advice, he shows an increased degree of reverence, but does not abandon his purpose; and should they punish him, he does not allow himself to murmur."

CHAPTER XIX. The Master said, "While his parents are alive, the son may not go abroad to a distance. If he does go abroad, he must have a fixed place to which he goes."

CHAPTER XX. The Master said, "If the son for three years does not alter from the way of his father, he may be called filial."

CHAPTER XXI. The Master said, "The years of parents may by no means not be kept in the memory, as an occasion at once for joy and for fear."

CHAPTER XXII. The Master said, "The reason why the ancients did not readily give utterance to their words was that they feared lest their actions should not come up to them."

CHAPTER XXIII. The Master said, "The cautious seldom err."

CHAPTER XXIV. The Master said, "The superior man wishes to be slow in his speech and earnest in his conduct."

CHAPTER XXV. The Master said, "Virtue is not left to stand alone. He who practises it will have neighbors."

CHAPTER XXVI. Tsze-yu said, "In serving a prince, frequent remonstrances lead to disgrace. Between friends, frequent reproofs make the friendship distant."

Book V

KUNG-YE CH'ANG

CHAPTER I. 1. The Master said of Kung-ye Ch'ang that he might be wived; although he was put in bonds, he had not been guilty of any crime. Accordingly, he gave him his own daughter to wife.

2. Of Nan Yung he said that if the country were well-governed he would not be out of office, and if it were ill-governed, he would escape punishment and disgrace. He gave him the daughter of his own elder brother to wife.

CHAPTER II. The Master said of Tsze-chien, "Of superior virtue indeed is such a man! If there were not virtuous men in Lu, how could this man have acquired this character?"

CHAPTER III. Tsze-kung asked, "What do you say of me, Ts'ze?" The Master said, "You are a utensil." "What utensil?" "A gemmed sacrificial utensil."

CHAPTER IV. 1. Someone said, "Yung is truly virtuous, but he is not ready with his tongue."

2. The Master said, "What is the good of being ready with the tongue? They who encounter men with smartnesses of speech for the most part procure themselves hatred. I know not whether he be truly virtuous, but why should he show readiness of the tongue?"

CHAPTER V. The Master was wishing Ch'i-tiao K'ai to enter an official employment. He replied, "I am not yet able to rest in the assurance of THIS." The Master was pleased.

CHAPTER VI. The Master said, "My doctrines make no way. I will get upon a raft, and float about on the sea. He that will accompany me will be Yu, I dare say." Tsze-lu hearing this was glad, upon which the Master said, "Yu is fonder of daring than I am. He does not exercise his judgment upon matters."

CHAPTER VII. 1. Mang Wu asked about Tsze-lu, whether he was perfectly virtuous. The Master said, "I do not know."

2. He asked again, when the Master replied, "In a kingdom of a thousand chariots, Yu might be employed to manage the military levies, but I do not know whether he be perfectly virtuous."

3. "And what do you say of Ch'iu?" The Master replied, "In a city of a thousand families, or a clan of a hundred chariots, Ch'iu might be employed as governor, but I do not know whether he is perfectly virtuous."

4. "What do you say of Ch'ih?" The Master replied, "With his sash girt and standing in a court, Ch'ih might be employed to converse with the visitors and guests, but I do not know whether he is perfectly virtuous."

CHAPTER VIII. 1. The Master said to Tsze-kung, "Which do you consider superior, yourself or Hui?"

2. Tsze-kung replied, "How dare I compare myself with Hui? Hui hears one point and knows all about a subject; I hear one point, and know a second."

3. The Master said, "You are not equal to him. I grant you, you are not equal to him."

CHAPTER IX. 1. Tsai Yu being asleep during the daytime, the Master said, "Rotten wood cannot be carved; a wall of dirty earth will not receive the trowel. This Yu! What is the use of my reproving him?"

2. The Master said, "At first, my way with men was to hear their words, and give them credit for their conduct. Now my way is to hear their words, and look at their conduct. It is from Yu that I have learned to make this change."

CHAPTER X. The Master said, "I have not seen a firm and unbending man." Someone replied, "There is Shan Ch'ang." "Ch'ang," said the Master, "is under the influence of his passions; how can he be pronounced firm and unbending?"

CHAPTER XI. Tsze-kung said, "What I do not wish men to do to me, I also wish not to do to men." The Master said, "Ts'ze, you have not attained to that."

CHAPTER XII. Tsze-kung said, "The Master's personal displays of his principles and ordinary descriptions of them may be heard. His discourses about man's nature, and the Way of Heaven, cannot be heard."

CHAPTER XIII. When Tsze-lu heard anything, if he had not yet succeeded in carrying it into practice, he was only afraid lest he should hear something else.

CHAPTER XIV. Tsze-kung asked, saying, "On what ground did Kung-wan get that title of Wan?" The Master said, "He was of an active nature and yet fond of learning, and he was not ashamed to ask and learn of his inferiors! On these grounds he has been styled Wan."

CHAPTER XV. The Master said of Tsze-ch'an that he had four of the characteristics of a superior man: in his conduct of himself, he was humble; in serving his superiors, he was respectful; in nourishing the people, he was kind; in ordering the people, he was just.

CHAPTER XVI. The Master said, "Yen P'ing knew well how to maintain friendly intercourse. The acquaintance might be long, but he showed the same respect as at first."

CHAPTER XVII. The Master said, "Tsang Wan kept a large tortoise in a house, on the capitals of the pillars of which he had hills made, and with representations of duckweed on the small pillars above the beams supporting the rafters. Of what sort was his wisdom?"

CHAPTER XVIII. 1. Tsze-chang asked, saying, "The minister Tsze-wan thrice took office, and manifested no joy in his countenance. Thrice he retired from office, and manifested no displeasure. He made it a point to inform the new minister of the way in which he had conducted the government; what do you say of him?" The Master replied, "He was loyal." "Was he perfectly virtuous?" "I do not know. How can he be pronounced perfectly virtuous?"

2. Tsze-chang proceeded, "When the officer Ch'ui killed the prince of Ch'i, Ch'an Wan, though he was the owner of forty horses, abandoned them and left the country. Coming to another State, he said, 'They are here like our great officer, Ch'ui' and left it. He came to a second State, and with the same observation left it also; what do you say of him?" The Master replied, "He was pure." "Was he perfectly virtuous?" "I do not know. How can he be pronounced perfectly virtuous?"

CHAPTER XIX. Chi Wan thought thrice, and then acted. When the Master was informed of it, he said, "Twice may do."

CHAPTER XX. The Master said, "When good order prevailed in his country, Ning Wu acted the part of a wise man. When his country was in disorder, he acted the part of a stupid man. Others may equal his wisdom, but they cannot equal his stupidity."

CHAPTER XXI. When the Master was in Ch'an, he said, "Let me return! Let me return! The little children of my school are ambitious and too hasty. They are accomplished and complete so far, but they do not know how to restrict and shape themselves."

CHAPTER XXII. The Master said, "Po-i and Shu-ch'i did not keep the former wickednesses of men in mind, and hence the resentments directed towards them were few."

CHAPTER XXIII. The Master said, "Who says of Wei-shang Kao that he is upright? One begged some vinegar of him, and he begged it of a neighbor and gave it to the man."

CHAPTER XXIV. The Master said, "Fine words, an insinuating appearance, and excessive respect; Tso Ch'iu-ming was ashamed of them. I also am ashamed of them. To conceal resentment against a person, and appear friendly with him; Tso Ch'iu-ming was ashamed of such conduct. I also am ashamed of it."

CHAPTER XXV. 1. Yen Yuan and Chi Lu being by his side, the Master said to them, "Come, let each of you tell his wishes."

2. Tsze-lu said, "I should like, having chariots and horses, and light fur dresses, to share them with my friends, and though they should spoil them, I would not be displeased."

3. Yen Yuan said, "I should like not to boast of my excellence, nor to make a display of my meritorious deeds."

4. Tsze-lu then said, "I should like, sir, to hear your wishes." The Master said, "They are, in regard to the aged, to give them rest; in regard to friends, to show them sincerity; in regard to the young, to treat them tenderly."

CHAPTER XXVI. The Master said, "It is all over! I have not yet seen one who could perceive his faults, and inwardly accuse himself."

CHAPTER XXVII. The Master said, "In a hamlet of ten families, there may be found one honourable and sincere as I am, but not so fond of learning."

Book VI

YUNG YEY

CHAPTER I. 1. The Master said, "There is Yung! He might occupy the place of a prince."

2. Chung-kung asked about Tsze-sang Po-tsze. The Master said, "He may pass. He does not mind small matters."

3. Chung-kung said, "If a man cherish in himself a reverential feeling of the necessity of attention to business, though he may be easy in small matters in his government of the people, that may be allowed. But if he cherish in himself that easy feeling, and also carry it out in his practice, is not such an easy mode of procedure excessive?"

4. The Master said, "Yung's words are right."

CHAPTER II. The Duke Ai asked which of the disciples loved to learn. Confucius replied to him, "There was Yen Hui; HE loved to learn. He did not transfer his anger; he did not repeat a fault.

Unfortunately, his appointed time was short and he died; and now there is not such another. I have not yet heard of anyone who loves to learn as he did."

CHAPTER III. 1. Tsze-hwa being employed on a mission to Ch'i, the disciple Zan requested grain for his mother. The Master said, "Give her a fu." Yen requested more. "Give her an yu," said the Master. Yen gave her five ping.

2. The Master said, "When Ch'ih was proceeding to Ch'i, he had fat horses to his carriage, and wore light furs. I have heard that a superior man helps the distressed, but does not add to the wealth of the rich."

3. Yuan Sze being made governor of his town by the Master, he gave him nine hundred measures of grain, but Sze declined them.

4. The Master said, "Do not decline them. May you not give them away in the neighborhoods, hamlets, towns, and villages?"

CHAPTER IV. The Master, speaking of Chung-kung, said, "If the calf of a brindled cow be red and horned, although men may not wish to use it, would the spirits of the mountains and rivers put it aside?"

CHAPTER V. The Master said, "Such was Hui that for three months there would be nothing in his mind contrary to perfect virtue. The others may attain to this on some days or in some months, but nothing more."

CHAPTER VI. Chi K'ang asked about Chung-yu, whether he was fit to be employed as an officer of government. The Master said,

"Yu is a man of decision; what difficulty would he find in being an officer of government?" K'ang asked, "Is Ts'ze fit to be employed as an officer of government?" and was answered, "Ts'ze is a man of intelligence; what difficulty would he find in being an officer of government?" And to the same question about Ch'iu the Master gave the same reply, saying, "Ch'iu is a man of various ability."

CHAPTER VII. The chief of the Chi family sent to ask Min Tsze-ch'ien to be governor of Pi. Min Tsze-ch'ien said, "Decline the offer for me politely. If anyone come again to me with a second invitation, I shall be obliged to go and live on the banks of the Wan."

CHAPTER VIII. Po-niu being ill, the Master went to ask for him. He took hold of his hand through the window, and said, "It is killing him. It is the appointment of Heaven, alas! That such a man should have such a sickness! That such a man should have such a sickness!"

CHAPTER IX. The Master said, "Admirable indeed was the virtue of Hui! With a single bamboo dish of rice, a single gourd dish of drink, and living in his mean narrow lane, while others could not have endured the distress, he did not allow his joy to be affected by it. Admirable indeed was the virtue of Hui!"

CHAPTER X. Yen Ch'iu said, "It is not that I do not delight in your doctrines, but my strength is insufficient." The Master said, "Those whose strength is insufficient give over in the middle of the way but now you limit yourself."

CHAPTER XI. The Master said to Tsze-hsia, "Do you be a scholar after the style of the superior man, and not after that of the mean man."

CHAPTER XII. Tsze-yu being governor of Wu-ch'ang, the Master said to him, "Have you got good men there?" He answered, "There is Tan-t'ai Mieh-ming, who never in walking takes a shortcut, and never comes to my office, excepting on public business."

CHAPTER XIII. The Master said, "Mang Chih-fan does not boast of his merit. Being in the rear on an occasion of flight, when they were about to enter the gate, he whipped up his horse, saying, 'It is not that I dare to be last. My horse would not advance.' "

CHAPTER XIV. The Master said, "Without the specious speech of the litanist T'o and the beauty of the prince Chao of Sung, it is difficult to escape in the present age."

CHAPTER XV. The Master said, "Who can go out but by the door? How is it that men will not walk according to these ways?"

CHAPTER XVI. The Master said, "Where the solid qualities are in excess of accomplishments, we have rusticity; where the accomplishments are in excess of the solid qualities, we have the manners of a clerk. When the accomplishments and solid qualities are equally blended, we then have the man of virtue."

CHAPTER XVII. The Master said, "Man is born for uprightness. If a man lose his uprightness, and yet live, his escape from death is the effect of mere good fortune."

CHAPTER XVIII. The Master said, "They who know the truth are not equal to those who love it, and they who love it are not equal to those who delight in it."

CHAPTER XIX. The Master said, "To those whose talents are above mediocrity, the highest subjects may be announced. To those who are below mediocrity, the highest subjects may not be announced."

CHAPTER XX. Fan Ch'ih asked what constituted wisdom. The Master said, "To give one's self earnestly to the duties due to men, and, while respecting spiritual beings, to keep aloof from them, may be called wisdom." He asked about perfect virtue. The Master said, "The man of virtue makes the difficulty to be overcome his first business, and success only a subsequent consideration—this may be called perfect virtue."

CHAPTER XXI. The Master said, "The wise find pleasure in water; the virtuous find pleasure in hills. The wise are active; the virtuous are tranquil. The wise are joyful; the virtuous are long-lived."

CHAPTER XXII. The Master said, "Ch'i, by one change, would come to the State of Lu. Lu, by one change, would come to a State where true principles predominated."

CHAPTER XXIII. The Master said, "A cornered vessel without corners—A strange cornered vessel! A strange cornered vessel!"

CHAPTER XXIV. Tsai Wo asked, saying, "A benevolent man, though it be told him 'There is a man in the well,' will go in after him, I suppose." Confucius said, "Why should he do so? A superior man may be made to go to the well, but he cannot be made to go down into it. He may be imposed upon, but he cannot be fooled."

CHAPTER XXV. The Master said, "The superior man, extensively studying all learning, and keeping himself under the restraint of the rules of propriety, may thus likewise not overstep what is right."

CHAPTER XXVI. The Master having visited Nan-tsze, Tsze-lu was displeased, on which the Master swore, saying, "Wherein I have done improperly, may Heaven reject me, may Heaven reject me!"

CHAPTER XXVII. The Master said, "Perfect is the virtue which is according to the Constant Mean! Rare for a long time has been its practice among the people."

CHAPTER XXVIII. 1. Tsze-kung said, "Suppose the case of a man extensively conferring benefits on the people, and able to assist all, what would you say of him? Might he be called perfectly virtuous?" The Master said, "Why speak only of virtue in connection with him? Must he not have the qualities of a sage? Even Yao and Shun were still solicitous about this.

2. "Now the man of perfect virtue, wishing to be established himself, seeks also to establish others; wishing to be enlarged himself, he seeks also to enlarge others.

3. "To be able to judge of others by what is nigh in ourselves— this may be called the art of virtue."

Book VII

SHU R

CHAPTER I. The Master said, "A transmitter and not a maker, believing in and loving the ancients, I venture to compare myself with our old P'ang."

CHAPTER II. The Master said, "The silent treasuring up of knowledge; learning without satiety; and instructing others without being wearied: which one of these things belongs to me?"

CHAPTER III. The Master said, "The leaving virtue without proper cultivation; the not thoroughly discussing what is learned; not being able to move towards righteousness of which a knowledge is gained; and not being able to change what is not good: these are the things which occasion me solicitude."

CHAPTER IV. When the Master was unoccupied with business, his manner was easy, and he looked pleased.

CHAPTER V. The Master said, "Extreme is my decay. For a long time, I have not dreamed, as I was wont to do, that I saw the Duke of Chau."

CHAPTER VI. 1. The Master said, "Let the will be set on the path of duty.

2. "Let every attainment in what is good be firmly grasped.

3. "Let perfect virtue be accorded with.

4. "Let relaxation and enjoyment be found in the polite arts."

CHAPTER VII. The Master said, "From the man bringing his bundle of dried flesh for my teaching upwards, I have never refused instruction to anyone."

CHAPTER VIII. The Master said, "I do not open up the truth to one who is not eager to get knowledge, nor help out anyone who is not anxious to explain himself. When I have presented one corner of a subject to anyone, and he cannot from it learn the other three, I do not repeat my lesson."

CHAPTER IX. 1. When the Master was eating by the side of a mourner, he never ate to the full.

2. He did not sing on the same day in which he had been weeping.

CHAPTER X. 1. The Master said to Yen Yuan, "When called to office, to undertake its duties; when not so called, to lie retired—it is only I and you who have attained to this."

2. Tsze-lu said, "If you had the conduct of the armies of a great State, whom would you have to act with you?"

3. The Master said, "I would not have him to act with me who will unarmed attack a tiger, or cross a river without a boat, dying without any regret. My associate must be the man who proceeds to action full of solicitude, who is fond of adjusting his plans, and then carries them into execution."

CHAPTER XI. The Master said, "If the search for riches is sure to be successful, though I should become a groom with whip in hand to get them, I will do so. As the search may not be successful, I will follow after that which I love."

CHAPTER XII. The things in reference to which the Master exercised the greatest caution were—fasting, war, and sickness.

CHAPTER XIII. When the Master was in Ch'i, he heard the Shao, and for three months did not know the taste of flesh. "I did not think," he said, "that music could have been made so excellent as this."

CHAPTER XIV. 1. Yen Yu said, "Is our Master for the ruler of Wei?" Tsze-kung said, "Oh! I will ask him."

2. He went in accordingly, and said, "What sort of men were Po-i and Shu-ch'i?" "They were ancient worthies," said the Master. "Did they have any repinings because of their course?" The Master again replied, "They sought to act virtuously, and they did so; what was there for them to repine about?" On this, Tsze-kung went out and said, "Our Master is not for him."

CHAPTER XV. The Master said, "With coarse rice to eat, with water to drink, and my bended arm for a pillow—I have still joy in the midst of these things. Riches and honours acquired by unrighteousness are to me as a floating cloud."

CHAPTER XVI. The Master said, "If some years were added to my life, I would give fifty to the study of the Yi, and then I might come to be without great faults."

CHAPTER XVII The Master's frequent themes of discourse were—the Odes, the History, and the maintenance of the Rules of Propriety. On all these he frequently discoursed.

CHAPTER XVIII. 1. The Duke of Sheh asked Tsze-lu about Confucius, and Tsze-lu did not answer him.

2. The Master said, "Why did you not say to him, He is simply a man, who in his eager pursuit of knowledge forgets his food, who in the joy of its attainment forgets his sorrows, and who does not perceive that old age is coming on?"

CHAPTER XIX. The Master said, "I am not one who was born in the possession of knowledge; I am one who is fond of antiquity, and earnest in seeking it there."

CHAPTER XX. The subjects on which the Master did not talk were—extraordinary things, feats of strength, disorder, and spiritual beings.

CHAPTER XXI. The Master said, "When I walk along with two others, they may serve me as my teachers. I will select their good qualities and follow them, their bad qualities and avoid them."

CHAPTER XXII. The Master said, "Heaven produced the virtue that is in me. Hwan T'ui—what can he do to me?"

CHAPTER XXIII. The Master said, "Do you think, my disciples, that I have any concealments? I conceal nothing from you. There is nothing which I do that is not shown to you, my disciples; that is my way."

CHAPTER XXIV. There were four things which the Master taught—letters, ethics, devotion of soul, and truthfulness.

CHAPTER XXV. 1. The Master said, "A sage it is not mine to see; could I see a man of real talent and virtue, that would satisfy me."

2. The Master said, "A good man it is not mine to see; could I see a man possessed of constancy, that would satisfy me.

3. "Having not and yet affecting to have, empty and yet affecting to be full, straitened and yet affecting to be at ease: it is difficult with such characteristics to have constancy."

CHAPTER XXVI. The Master angled—but did not use a net. He shot—but not at birds perching.

CHAPTER XXVII. The Master said, "There may be those who act without knowing why. I do not do so. Hearing much and selecting what is good and following it; seeing much and keeping it in memory: this is the second style of knowledge."

CHAPTER XXVIII. 1. It was difficult to talk profitably and reputably with the people of Hu-hsiang, and a lad of that place having had an interview with the Master, the disciples doubted.

2. The Master said, "I admit people's approach to me without committing myself as to what they may do when they have retired. Why must one be so severe? If a man purify himself to

wait upon me, I receive him so purified, without guaranteeing his past conduct."

CHAPTER XXIX. The Master said, "Is virtue a thing remote? I wish to be virtuous, and lo! Virtue is at hand."

CHAPTER XXX. 1. The minister of crime of Ch'an asked whether the Duke Chao knew propriety, and Confucius said, "He knew propriety."

2. Confucius having retired, the minister bowed to Wu-ma Ch'i to come forward, and said, "I have heard that the superior man is not a partisan. May the superior man be a partisan also? The prince married a daughter of the house of Wu, of the same surname with himself, and called her 'The elder Tsze of Wu' If the prince knew propriety, who does not know it?"

3. Wu-ma Ch'i reported these remarks, and the Master said, "I am fortunate! If I have any errors, people are sure to know them."

CHAPTER XXXI. When the Master was in company with a person who was singing, if he sang well, he would make him repeat the song, while he accompanied it with his own voice.

CHAPTER XXXII. The Master said, "In letters I am perhaps equal to other men, but the character of the superior man, carrying out in his conduct what he professes, is what I have not yet attained to."

CHAPTER XXXIII. The Master said, "The sage and the man of perfect virtue—how dare I rank myself with them? It may simply be said of me that I strive to become such without satiety, and teach others without weariness." Kung-hsi Hwa said, "This is just what we, the disciples, cannot imitate you in."

CHAPTER XXXIV. The Master being very sick, Tsze-lu asked leave to pray for him. He said, "May such a thing be done?" Tsze-lu replied, "It may. In the Eulogies it is said, 'Prayer has been made for thee to the spirits of the upper and lower worlds.'" The Master said, "My praying has been for a long time."

CHAPTER XXXV. The Master said, "Extravagance leads to insubordination, and parsimony to meanness. It is better to be mean than to be insubordinate."

CHAPTER XXXVI. The Master said, "The superior man is satisfied and composed; the mean man is always full of distress."

CHAPTER XXXVII. The Master was mild, and yet dignified; majestic, and yet not fierce; respectful, and yet easy.

Book VIII

T'AI-PO

CHAPTER I. The Master said, "T'ai-po may be said to have reached the highest point of virtuous action. Thrice he declined the kingdom, and the people in ignorance of his motives could not express their approbation of his conduct."

CHAPTER II. 1. The Master said, "Respectfulness, without the rules of propriety, becomes laborious bustle; carefulness, without the rules of propriety, becomes timidity; boldness, without the rules of propriety, becomes insubordination; straightforwardness, without the rules of propriety, becomes rudeness.

2. "When those who are in high stations perform well all their duties to their relations, the people are aroused to virtue. When old friends are not neglected by them, the people are preserved from meanness."

CHAPTER III. The philosopher Tsang being ill, he called to him the disciples of his school, and said, "Uncover my feet, uncover my hands. It is said in the 'Book of Poetry,' 'We should be apprehensive and cautious, as if on the brink of a deep gulf, as if treading on thin ice,' and so have I been. Now and hereafter, I know my escape from all injury to my person, O ye, my little children."

CHAPTER IV. 1. The philosopher Tsang being ill, Meng Chang went to ask how he was.

2. Tsang said to him, "When a bird is about to die, its notes are mournful; when a man is about to die, his words are good.

3. "There are three principles of conduct which the man of high rank should consider specially important: that in his deportment and manner he keep from violence and heedlessness; that in regulating his countenance he keep near to sincerity; and that in his words and tones he keep far from lowness and impropriety. As to such matters as attending to the sacrificial vessels, there are the proper officers for them."

CHAPTER V. The philosopher Tsang said, "Gifted with ability, and yet putting questions to those who were not so; possessed of much, and yet putting questions to those possessed of little; having, as though he had not; full, and yet counting himself as empty; offended against, and yet entering into no altercation; formerly I had a friend who pursued this style of conduct."

CHAPTER VI. The philosopher Tsang said, "Suppose that there is an individual who can be entrusted with the charge of a young orphan prince, and can be commissioned with authority over a State of a hundred li, and whom no emergency however great can drive from his principles: is such a man a superior man? He is a superior man indeed."

CHAPTER VII. 1. The philosopher Tsang said, "The officer may not be without breadth of mind and vigorous endurance. His burden is heavy and his course is long.

2. "Perfect virtue is the burden which he considers it is his to sustain; is it not heavy? Only with death does his course stop; is it not long?

CHAPTER VIII. 1. The Master said, "It is by the Odes that the mind is aroused.

2. "It is by the Rules of Propriety that the character is established.

3. "It is from Music that the finish is received."

CHAPTER IX. The Master said, "The people may be made to follow a path of action, but they may not be made to understand it."

CHAPTER X. The Master said, "The man who is fond of daring and is dissatisfied with poverty will proceed to insubordination. So will the man who is not virtuous, when you carry your dislike of him to an extreme."

CHAPTER XI. The Master said, "Though a man have abilities as admirable as those of the Duke of Chau, yet if he be proud and niggardly, those other things are really not worth being looked at."

CHAPTER XII. The Master said, "It is not easy to find a man who has learned for three years without coming to be good."

CHAPTER XIII. 1. The Master said, "With sincere faith he unites the love of learning; holding firm to death, he is perfecting the excellence of his course.

2. "Such an one will not enter a tottering State, nor dwell in a disorganized one. When right principles of government prevail in the kingdom, he will show himself; when they are prostrated, he will keep concealed.

3. "When a country is well-governed, poverty and a mean condition are things to be ashamed of. When a country is ill-governed, riches and honour are things to be ashamed of."

CHAPTER XIV. The Master said, "He who is not in any particular office has nothing to do with plans for the administration of its duties."

CHAPTER XV. The Master said, "When the music master Chih first entered on his office, the finish of the Kwan Tsu was magnificent—how it filled the ears!"

CHAPTER XVI. The Master said, "Ardent and yet not upright; stupid and yet not attentive; simple and yet not sincere: such persons I do not understand."

CHAPTER XVII. The Master said, "Learn as if you could not reach your object, and were always fearing also lest you should lose it."

CHAPTER XVIII. The Master said, "How majestic was the manner in which Shun and Yu held possession of the empire, as if it were nothing to them!"

CHAPTER XIX. 1. The Master said, "Great indeed was Yao as a sovereign! How majestic was he! It is only Heaven that is grand, and only Yao corresponded to it. How vast was his virtue! The people could find no name for it.

2. "How majestic was he in the works which he accomplished! How glorious in the elegant regulations which he instituted!"

CHAPTER XX. 1. Shun had five ministers, and the empire was well-governed.

2. King Wu said, "I have ten able ministers."

3. Confucius said, "Is not the saying that talents are difficult to find true? Only when the dynasties of T'ang and Yu met were they more abundant than in this of Chau, yet there was a woman among them. The able ministers were no more than nine men.

4. "King Wan possessed two of the three parts of the empire, and with those he served the dynasty of Yin. The virtue of the house of Chau may be said to have reached the highest point indeed."

CHAPTER XXI. The Master said, "I can find no flaw in the character of Yu. He used himself coarse food and drink, but displayed the utmost filial piety towards the spirits. His ordinary garments were poor, but he displayed the utmost elegance in his sacrificial cap and apron. He lived in a low mean house, but expended all his strength on the ditches and water-channels. I can find nothing like a flaw in Yu."

Book IX

TSZE HAN

CHAPTER I. The subjects of which the Master seldom spoke were—profitableness, and also the appointments of Heaven, and perfect virtue.

CHAPTER II. 1. A man of the village of Ta-hsiang said, "Great indeed is the philosopher K'ung! His learning is extensive, and yet he does not render his name famous by any particular thing."

2. The Master heard the observation, and said to his disciples, "What shall I practise? Shall I practise charioteering, or shall I practise archery? I will practise charioteering."

CHAPTER III. 1. The Master said, "The linen cap is that prescribed by the rules of ceremony, but now a silk one is worn. It is economical, and I follow the common practice.

2. "The rules of ceremony prescribe the bowing below the hall, but now the practice is to bow only after ascending it. That is

arrogant. I continue to bow below the hall, though I oppose the common practice."

CHAPTER IV. There were four things from which the Master was entirely free. He had no foregone conclusions, no arbitrary predeterminations, no obstinacy, and no egoism.

CHAPTER V. 1. The Master was put in fear in K'wang.

2. He said, "After the death of King Wan, was not the cause of truth lodged here in me?

3. "If Heaven had wished to let this cause of truth perish, then I, a future mortal, should not have got such a relation to that cause. While Heaven does not let the cause of truth perish, what can the people of K'wang do to me?"

CHAPTER VI. 1. A high officer asked Tsze-kung, saying, "May we not say that your Master is a sage? How various is his ability!"

2. Tsze-kung said, "Certainly Heaven has endowed him unlimitedly. He is about a sage. And, moreover, his ability is various."

3. The Master heard of the conversation and said, "Does the high officer know me? When I was young, my condition was low, and therefore I acquired my ability in many things, but they were mean matters. Must the superior man have such variety of ability? He does not need variety of ability."

4. Lao said, "The Master said, 'Having no official employment, I acquired many arts.' "

CHAPTER VII. The Master said, "Am I indeed possessed of knowledge? I am not knowing. But if a mean person, who appears quite empty-like, ask anything of me, I set it forth from one end to the other, and exhaust it."

CHAPTER VIII. The Master said, "The FANG bird does not come; the river sends forth no map—it is all over with me!"

CHAPTER IX. When the Master saw a person in a mourning dress, or anyone with the cap and upper and lower garments of full dress, or a blind person, on observing them approaching, though they were younger than himself, he would rise up, and if he had to pass by them, he would do so hastily.

CHAPTER X. 1. Yen Yuan, in admiration of the Master's doctrines, sighed and said, "I looked up to them, and they seemed to become more high; I tried to penetrate them, and they seemed to become more firm; I looked at them before me, and suddenly they seemed to be behind.

2. "The Master, by orderly method, skilfully leads men on. He enlarged my mind with learning, and taught me the restraints of propriety.

3. "When I wish to give over the study of his doctrines, I cannot do so, and having exerted all my ability, there seems something to stand right up before me; but though I wish to follow and lay hold of it, I really find no way to do so."

CHAPTER XI. 1. The Master being very ill, Tsze-lu wished the disciples to act as ministers to him.

2. During a remission of his illness, he said, "Long has the conduct of Yu been deceitful! By pretending to have ministers when I have them not, whom should I impose upon? Should I impose upon Heaven?

3. "Moreover, than that I should die in the hands of ministers, is it not better that I should die in the hands of you, my disciples? And though I may not get a great burial, shall I die upon the road?"

CHAPTER XII. Tsze-kung said, "There is a beautiful gem here. Should I lay it up in a case and keep it? Or should I seek for a good price and sell it?" The Master said, "Sell it! Sell it! But I would wait for one to offer the price."

CHAPTER XIII. 1. The Master was wishing to go and live among the nine wild tribes of the east.

2. Someone said, "They are rude. How can you do such a thing?" The Master said, "If a superior man dwelt among them, what rudeness would there be?"

CHAPTER XIV. The Master said, "I returned from Wei to Lu, and then the music was reformed, and the pieces in the Royal songs and Praise songs all found their proper places."

CHAPTER XV. The Master said, "Abroad, to serve the high ministers and nobles; at home, to serve one's father and elder brothers; in all duties to the dead, not to dare not to exert one's self; and not to be overcome of wine: which one of these things do I attain to?"

CHAPTER XVI. The Master standing by a stream, said, "It passes on just like this, not ceasing day or night!"

CHAPTER XVII. The Master said, "I have not seen one who loves virtue as he loves beauty."

CHAPTER XVIII. The Master said, "The prosecution of learning may be compared to what may happen in raising a mound. If there want but one basket of earth to complete the work, and I stop, the stopping is my own work. It may be compared to throwing down the earth on the level ground. Though but one basketful is thrown at a time, the advancing with it is my own going forward."

CHAPTER XIX. The Master said, "Never flagging when I set forth anything to him—ah! That is Hui."

CHAPTER XX. The Master said of Yen Yuan, "Alas! I saw his constant advance. I never saw him stop in his progress."

CHAPTER XXI. The Master said, "There are cases in which the blade springs, but the plant does not go on to flower! There are cases where it flowers, but no fruit is subsequently produced!"

CHAPTER XXII. The Master said, "A youth is to be regarded with respect. How do we know that his future will not be equal to our present? If he reach the age of forty or fifty, and has not made himself heard of, then indeed he will not be worth being regarded with respect."

CHAPTER XXIII. The Master said, "Can men refuse to assent to the words of strict admonition? But it is reforming the conduct because of them which is valuable. Can men refuse to be pleased with words of gentle advice? But it is unfolding their aim which is valuable. If a man be pleased with these words, but does not unfold their aim, and assents to those, but does not reform his conduct, I can really do nothing with him."

CHAPTER XXIV. The Master said, "Hold faithfulness and sincerity as first principles. Have no friends not equal to yourself. When you have faults, do not fear to abandon them."

CHAPTER XXV. The Master said, "The commander of the forces of a large State may be carried off, but the will of even a common man cannot be taken from him."

CHAPTER XXVI. 1. The Master said, "Dressed himself in a tattered robe quilted with hemp, yet standing by the side of men dressed in furs, and not ashamed—ah! It is Yu who is equal to this!

2. " 'He dislikes none, he covets nothing; what can he do but what is good!' "

3. Tsze-lu kept continually repeating these words of the ode, when the Master said, "Those things are by no means sufficient to constitute perfect excellence."

CHAPTER XXVII. The Master said, "When the year becomes cold, then we know how the pine and the cypress are the last to lose their leaves."

CHAPTER XXVIII. The Master said, "The wise are free from perplexities; the virtuous from anxiety; and the bold from fear."

CHAPTER XXIX. The Master said, "There are some with whom we may study in common, but we shall find them unable to go along with us to principles. Perhaps we may go on with them to principles, but we shall find them unable to get established in those along with us. Or if we may get so established along with them, we shall find them unable to weigh occurring events along with us."

CHAPTER XXX. 1. How the flowers of the aspen-plum flutter and turn! Do I not think of you? But your house is distant.

2. The Master said, "It is the want of thought about it. How is it distant?"

Book X

HEANG TANG

CHAPTER I. 1. Confucius, in his village, looked simple and sincere, and as if he were not able to speak.

2. When he was in the prince's ancestorial temple, or in the court, he spoke minutely on every point, but cautiously.

CHAP II. 1. When he was waiting at court, in speaking with the great officers of the lower grade, he spoke freely, but in a straightforward manner; in speaking with those of the higher grade, he did so blandly, but precisely.

2. When the ruler was present, his manner displayed respectful uneasiness; it was grave, but self-possessed.

CHAPTER III. 1. When the prince called him to employ him in the reception of a visitor, his countenance appeared to change, and his legs to move forward with difficulty.

2. He inclined himself to the other officers among whom he stood, moving his left or right arm, as their position required,

but keeping the skirts of his robe before and behind evenly adjusted.

3. He hastened forward, with his arms like the wings of a bird.

4. When the guest had retired, he would report to the prince, "The visitor is not turning round any more."

CHAPTER IV. 1. When he entered the palace gate, he seemed to bend his body, as if it were not sufficient to admit him.

2. When he was standing, he did not occupy the middle of the gate-way; when he passed in or out, he did not tread upon the threshold.

3. When he was passing the vacant place of the prince, his countenance appeared to change, and his legs to bend under him, and his words came as if he hardly had breath to utter them.

4. He ascended the reception hall, holding up his robe with both his hands, and his body bent; holding in his breath also, as if he dared not breathe.

5. When he came out from the audience, as soon as he had descended one step, he began to relax his countenance, and had a satisfied look. When he had got to the bottom of the steps, he advanced rapidly to his place, with his arms like wings, and on occupying it, his manner still showed respectful uneasiness.

CHAPTER V. 1. When he was carrying the scepter of his ruler, he seemed to bend his body, as if he were not able to bear its weight. He did not hold it higher than the position of the hands in making a bow, nor lower than their position in giving anything to another. His countenance seemed to change, and look apprehensive, and he dragged his feet along as if they were held by something to the ground.

2. In presenting the presents with which he was charged, he wore a placid appearance.

3. At his private audience, he looked highly pleased.

CHAPTER VI. 1. The superior man did not use a deep purple, or a puce colour, in the ornaments of his dress.

2. Even in his undress, he did not wear anything of a red or reddish colour.

3. In warm weather, he had a single garment either of coarse or fine texture, but he wore it displayed over an inner garment.

4. Over lamb's fur he wore a garment of black; over fawn's fur one of white; and over fox's fur one of yellow.

5. The fur robe of his undress was long, with the right sleeve short.

6. He required his sleeping dress to be half as long again as his body.

7. When staying at home, he used thick furs of the fox or the badger.

8. When he put off mourning, he wore all the appendages of the girdle.

9. His under-garment, except when it was required to be of the curtain shape, was made of silk cut narrow above and wide below.

10. He did not wear lamb's fur or a black cap on a visit of condolence.

11. On the first day of the month he put on his court robes, and presented himself at court.

CHAPTER VII. 1. When fasting, he thought it necessary to have his clothes brightly clean and made of linen cloth.

2. When fasting, he thought it necessary to change his food, and also to change the place where he commonly sat in the apartment.

CHAPTER VIII. 1. He did not dislike to have his rice finely cleaned, nor to have his minced meat cut quite small.

2. He did not eat rice which had been injured by heat or damp and turned sour, nor fish or flesh which was gone. He did not eat what was discoloured, or what was of a bad flavour, nor anything which was ill-cooked, or was not in season.

3. He did not eat meat which was not cut properly, nor what was served without its proper sauce.

4. Though there might be a large quantity of meat, he would not allow what he took to exceed the due proportion for the rice. It was only in wine that he laid down no limit for himself, but he did not allow himself to be confused by it.

5. He did not partake of wine and dried meat bought in the market.

6. He was never without ginger when he ate.

7. He did not eat much.

8. When he had been assisting at the prince's sacrifice, he did not keep the flesh which he received overnight. The flesh of his family sacrifice he did not keep over three days. If kept over three days, people could not eat it.

9. When eating, he did not converse. When in bed, he did not speak.

10. Although his food might be coarse rice and vegetable soup, he would offer a little of it in sacrifice with a grave, respectful air.

CHAPTER IX. If his mat was not straight, he did not sit on it.

CHAPTER X. 1. When the villagers were drinking together, on those who carried staffs going out, he went out immediately after.

2. When the villagers were going through their ceremonies to drive away pestilential influences, he put on his court robes and stood on the eastern steps.

CHAPTER XI. 1. When he was sending complimentary inquiries to anyone in another State, he bowed twice as he escorted the messenger away.

2. Chi K'ang having sent him a present of physic, he bowed and received it, saying, "I do not know it. I dare not taste it."

CHAPTER XII. The stable being burned down when he was at court, on his return he said, "Has any man been hurt?" He did not ask about the horses.

CHAPTER XIII. 1. When the prince sent him a gift of cooked meat, he would adjust his mat, first taste it, and then give it away to others. When the prince sent him a gift of undressed meat, he would have it cooked, and offer it to the spirits of his ancestors. When the prince sent him a gift of a living animal, he would keep it alive.

2. When he was in attendance on the prince and joining in the entertainment, the prince only sacrificed. He first tasted everything.

3. When he was ill and the prince came to visit him, he had his head to the east, made his court robes be spread over him, and drew his girdle across them.

4. When the prince's order called him, without waiting for his carriage to be yoked, he went at once.

CHAPTER XIV. When he entered the ancestral temple of the State, he asked about everything.

CHAPTER XV. 1. When any of his friends died, if he had no relations who could be depended on for the necessary offices, he would say, "I will bury him."

2. When a friend sent him a present, though it might be a carriage and horses, he did not bow.

3. The only present for which he bowed was that of the flesh of sacrifice.

CHAPTER XVI. 1. In bed, he did not lie like a corpse. At home, he did not put on any formal deportment.

2. When he saw anyone in a mourning dress, though it might be an acquaintance, he would change countenance; when he saw

anyone wearing the cap of full dress, or a blind person, though he might be in his undress, he would salute them in a ceremonious manner.

3. To any person in mourning he bowed forward to the crossbar of his carriage; he bowed in the same way to anyone bearing the tables of population.

4. When he was at an entertainment where there was an abundance of provisions set before him, he would change countenance and rise up.

5. On a sudden clap of thunder, or a violent wind, he would change countenance.

CHAPTER XVII. 1. When he was about to mount his carriage, he would stand straight, holding the cord.

2. When he was in the carriage, he did not turn his head quite round, he did not talk hastily, he did not point with his hands.

CHAPTER XVIII. 1. Seeing the countenance, it instantly rises. It flies round, and by and by settles.

2. The Master said, "There is the hen-pheasant on the hill bridge. At its season! At its season!" Tsze-lu made a motion to it. Thrice it smelt him and then rose.

Book XI

HSIEN TSIN

CHAPTER I. 1. The Master said, "The men of former times, in the matters of ceremonies and music, were rustics, it is said, while the men of these latter times, in ceremonies and music, are accomplished gentlemen.

2. "If I have occasion to use those things, I follow the men of former times."

CHAPTER II. 1. The Master said, "Of those who were with me in Ch'an and Ts'ai, there are none to be found to enter my door."

2. Distinguished for their virtuous principles and practice, there were Yen Yuan, Min Tsze-ch'ien, Zan Po-niu, and Chung-kung; for their ability in speech, Tsai Wo and Tsze-kung; for their administrative talents, Zan Yu and Chi Lu; for their literary acquirements, Tsze-yu and Tsze-hsia.

CHAPTER III. The Master said, "Hui gives me no assistance. There is nothing that I say in which he does not delight."

CHAPTER IV. The Master said, "Filial indeed is Min Tsze-ch'ien! Other people say nothing of him different from the report of his parents and brothers."

CHAPTER V. Nan Yung was frequently repeating the lines about a white scepter stone. Confucius gave him the daughter of his elder brother to wife.

CHAPTER VI. Chi K'ang asked which of the disciples loved to learn. Confucius replied to him, "There was Yen Hui; he loved to learn. Unfortunately his appointed time was short, and he died. Now there is no one who loves to learn, as he did."

CHAPTER VII. 1. When Yen Yuan died, Yen Lu begged the carriage of the Master to sell and get an outer shell for his son's coffin.

2. The Master said, "Everyone calls his son his son, whether he has talents or has not talents. There was Li; when he died, he had a coffin but no outer shell. I would not walk on foot to get a shell for him, because, having followed in the rear of the great officers, it was not proper that I should walk on foot."

CHAPTER VIII. When Yen Yuan died, the Master said, "Alas! Heaven is destroying me! Heaven is destroying me!"

CHAPTER IX. 1. When Yen Yuan died, the Master bewailed him exceedingly, and the disciples who were with him, "Master, your grief is excessive!"

2. "Is it excessive?" said he.

3. "If I am not to mourn bitterly for this man, for whom should I mourn?"

CHAPTER X. 1. When Yen Yuan died, the disciples wished to give him a great funeral, and the Master said, "You may not do so."

2. The disciples did bury him in great style.

3. The Master said, "Hui behaved towards me as his father. I have not been able to treat him as my son. The fault is not mine; it belongs to you, O disciples."

CHAPTER XI. Chi Lu asked about serving the spirits of the dead. The Master said, "While you are not able to serve men, how can you serve their spirits?" Chi Lu added, "I venture to ask about death?" He was answered, "While you do not know life, how can you know about death?"

CHAPTER XII. 1. The disciple Min was standing by his side, looking bland and precise; Tsze-lu, looking bold and soldierly; Zan Yu and Tsze-kung, with a free and straightforward manner. The Master was pleased.

2. He said, "Yu, there! He will not die a natural death."

CHAPTER XIII. 1. Some parties in Lu were going to take down and rebuild the Long Treasury.

2. Min Tsze-ch'ien said, "Suppose it were to be repaired after its old style—why must it be altered and made anew?"

3. The Master said, "This man seldom speaks; when he does, he is sure to hit the point."

CHAPTER XIV. 1. The Master said, "What has the lute of Yu to do in my door?"

2. The other disciples began not to respect Tsze-lu. The Master said, "Yu has ascended to the hall, though he has not yet passed into the inner apartments."

CHAPTER XV. 1. Tsze-kung asked which of the two, Shih or Shang, was the superior. The Master said, "Shih goes beyond the due mean, and Shang does not come up to it."

2. "Then," said Tsze-kung, "the superiority is with Shih, I suppose."

3. The Master said, "To go beyond is as wrong as to fall short."

CHAPTER XVI. 1. The head of the Chi family was richer than the Duke of Chau had been, and yet Ch'iu collected his imposts for him, and increased his wealth.

2. The Master said, "He is no disciple of mine. My little children, beat the drum and assail him."

CHAPTER XVII. 1. Ch'ai is simple.

2. Shan is dull.

3. Shih is specious.

4. Yu is coarse.

CHAPTER XVIII. 1. The Master said, "There is Hui! He has nearly attained to perfect virtue. He is often in want.

2. "Ts'ze does not acquiesce in the appointments of Heaven, and his goods are increased by him. Yet his judgments are often correct."

CHAPTER XIX. Tsze-chang asked what were the characteristics of the GOOD man. The Master said, "He does not tread in the footsteps of others, but moreover, he does not enter the chamber of the sage."

CHAPTER XX. The Master said, "If, because a man's discourse appears solid and sincere, we allow him to be a good man, is he really a superior man? Or is his gravity only in appearance?"

CHAPTER XXI. Tsze-lu asked whether he should immediately carry into practice what he heard. The Master said, "There are your father and elder brothers to be consulted; why should you act on that principle of immediately carrying into practice what you hear?" Zan Yu asked the same, whether he should immediately carry into practice what he heard, and the Master answered, "Immediately carry into practice what you hear." Kung-hsi Hwa said, "Yu asked whether he should carry immediately into practice what he heard, and you said, 'There are your father and elder brothers to be consulted.' Ch'iu asked whether he should immediately carry into practice what he heard, and you said, 'Carry it immediately into practice.' I, Ch'ih, am perplexed, and venture to ask you for an explanation." The Master said, "Ch'iu is retiring and slow; therefore, I urged him forward. Yu has more than his own share of energy; therefore I kept him back."

CHAPTER XXII. The Master was put in fear in K'wang and Yen Yuan fell behind. The Master, on his rejoining him, said, "I thought you had died." Hui replied, "While you were alive, how should I presume to die?"

CHAPTER XXIII. 1. Chi Tsze-zan asked whether Chung Yu and Zan Ch'iu could be called great ministers.

2. The Master said, "I thought you would ask about some extraordinary individuals, and you only ask about Yu and Ch'iu!

3. "What is called a great minister is one who serves his prince according to what is right, and when he finds he cannot do so, retires.

4. "Now, as to Yu and Ch'iu, they may be called ordinary ministers."

5. Tsze-zan said, "Then they will always follow their chief—will they?"

6. The Master said, "In an act of parricide or regicide, they would not follow him."

CHAPTER XXIV. 1. Tsze-lu got Tsze-kao appointed governor of Pi.

2. The Master said, "You are injuring a man's son."

3. Tsze-lu said, "There are there common people and officers; there are the altars of the spirits of the land and grain. Why must one read books before he can be considered to have learned?"

4. The Master said, "It is on this account that I hate your glib-tongued people."

CHAPTER XXV. 1. Tsze-lu, Tsang Hsi, Zan Yu, and Kung-hsi Hwa were sitting by the Master.

2. He said to them, "Though I am a day or so older than you, do not think of that.

3. "From day to day you are saying, 'We are not known.' If some ruler were to know you, what would you like to do?"

4. Tsze-lu hastily and lightly replied, "Suppose the case of a State of ten thousand chariots; let it be straitened between other large States; let it be suffering from invading armies; and to this let there be added a famine in corn and in all vegetables: if I were entrusted with the government of it, in three years' time I could make the people to be bold, and to recognise the rules of righteous conduct." The Master smiled at him.

5. Turning to Zan Yu, he said, "Ch'iu, what are your wishes?" Ch'iu replied, "Suppose a State of sixty or seventy li square, or one of fifty or sixty, and let me have the government of it; in three years' time, I could make plenty to abound among the people. As to teaching them the principles of propriety, and music, I must wait for the rise of a superior man to do that."

6. "What are your wishes, Ch'ih?" said the Master next to Kung-hsi Hwa. Ch'ih replied, "I do not say that my ability extends to these things, but I should wish to learn them. At the services of the ancestral temple, and at the audiences of the princes with the sovereign, I should like, dressed in the dark square-made robe and the black linen cap, to act as a small assistant."

7. Last of all, the Master asked Tsang Hsi, "Tien, what are your wishes?" Tien, pausing as he was playing on his lute, while it was yet twanging, laid the instrument aside, and rose. "My wishes," he said, "are different from the cherished purposes of these three gentlemen." "What harm is there in that?" said the Master; "Do you also, as well as they, speak out your wishes." Tien then said, "In this, the last month of spring, with the dress of the season all complete, along with five or six young men who have assumed the cap, and six or seven boys, I would wash in the I, enjoy the breeze among the rain altars, and return home singing." The Master heaved a sigh and said, "I give my approval to Tien."

8. The three others having gone out, Tsang Hsi remained behind, and said, "What do you think of the words of these three friends?" The Master replied, "They simply told each one his wishes."

9. Hsi pursued, "Master, why did you smile at Yu?"

10. He was answered, "The management of a State demands the rules of propriety. His words were not humble; therefore I smiled at him."

11. Hsi again said, "But was it not a State which Ch'iu proposed for himself?" The reply was, "Yes; did you ever see a territory of sixty or seventy li, or one of fifty or sixty, which was not a State?"

12. Once more, Hsi inquired, "And was it not a State which Ch'ih proposed for himself?" The Master again replied, "Yes; who but princes have to do with ancestral temples, and with audiences but the sovereign? If Ch'ih were to be a small assistant in these services, who could be a great one?"

Book XII

YEN YUAN

CHAPTER I. 1. Yen Yuan asked about perfect virtue. The Master said, "To subdue one's self and return to propriety is perfect virtue. If a man can for one day subdue himself and return to propriety, all under Heaven will ascribe perfect virtue to him. Is the practice of perfect virtue from a man himself, or is it from others?"

2. Yen Yuan said, "I beg to ask the steps of that process." The Master replied, "Look not at what is contrary to propriety; listen not to what is contrary to propriety; speak not what is contrary to propriety; make no movement which is contrary to propriety." Yen Yuan then said, "Though I am deficient in intelligence and vigour, I will make it my business to practise this lesson."

CHAPTER II. Chung-kung asked about perfect virtue. The Master said, "It is, when you go abroad, to behave to everyone as if you were receiving a great guest; to employ the people as if you were assisting at a great sacrifice; not to do to others as you would not wish done to yourself; to have no murmuring against you in the country, and none in the family." Chung-kung said, "Though I am deficient in intelligence and vigour, I will make it my business to practise this lesson."

CHAPTER III. 1. Sze-ma Niu asked about perfect virtue.

2. The Master said, "The man of perfect virtue is cautious and slow in his speech."

3. "Cautious and slow in his speech!" said Niu, "Is this what is meant by perfect virtue?" The Master said, "When a man feels the difficulty of doing, can he be other than cautious and slow in speaking?"

CHAPTER IV. 1. Sze-ma Niu asked about the superior man. The Master said, "The superior man has neither anxiety nor fear."

2. "Being without anxiety or fear!" said Nui, "Does this constitute what we call the superior man?"

3. The Master said, "When internal examination discovers nothing wrong, what is there to be anxious about, what is there to fear?"

CHAPTER V. 1. Sze-ma Niu, full of anxiety, said, "Other men all have their brothers, I only have not."

2. Tsze-hsia said to him, "There is the following saying which I have heard:

3. " 'Death and life have their determined appointment; riches and honours depend upon Heaven.'

4. "Let the superior man never fail reverentially to order his own conduct, and let him be respectful to others and observant of propriety—then all within the four seas will be his brothers. What has the superior man to do with being distressed because he has no brothers?"

CHAPTER VI. Tsze-chang asked what constituted intelligence. The Master said, "He with whom neither slander that gradually soaks into the mind, nor statements that startle like a wound in the flesh, are successful, may be called intelligent indeed. Yea, he with whom neither soaking slander, nor startling statements, are successful, may be called farseeing."

CHAPTER VII. 1. Tsze-kung asked about government. The Master said, "The requisites of government are that there be sufficiency of food, sufficiency of military equipment, and the confidence of the people in their ruler."

2. Tsze-kung said, "If it cannot be helped, and one of these must be dispensed with, which of the three should be foregone first?" "The military equipment," said the Master.

3. Tsze-kung again asked, "If it cannot be helped, and one of the remaining two must be dispensed with, which of them should be foregone?" The Master answered, "Part with the food. From of old, death has been the lot of all men; but if the people have no faith in their rulers, there is no standing for the State."

CHAPTER VIII. 1. Chi Tsze-ch'ang said, "In a superior man it is only the substantial qualities which are wanted; why should we seek for ornamental accomplishments?"

2. Tsze-kung said, "Alas! Your words, sir, show you to be a superior man, but four horses cannot overtake the tongue.

3. "Ornament is as substance; substance is as ornament. The hide of a tiger or a leopard stripped of its hair is like the hide of a dog or a goat stripped of its hair."

CHAPTER IX. 1. The Duke Ai inquired of Yu Zo, saying, "The year is one of scarcity, and the returns for expenditure are not sufficient; what is to be done?"

2. Yu Zo replied to him, "Why not simply tithe the people?"

3. "With two-tenths," said the duke, "I find it not enough; how could I do with that system of one-tenth?"

4. Yu Zo answered, "If the people have plenty, their prince will not be left to want alone. If the people are in want, their prince cannot enjoy plenty alone."

CHAPTER X. 1. Tsze-chang having asked how virtue was to be exalted, and delusions to be discovered, the Master said, "Hold faithfulness and sincerity as first principles, and be moving continually to what is right; this is the way to exalt one's virtue.

2. "You love a man and wish him to live; you hate him and wish him to die. Having wished him to live, you also wish him to die. This is a case of delusion.

3. " 'It may not be on account of her being rich, yet you come to make a difference.' "

CHAPTER XI. 1. The Duke Ching, of Ch'i, asked Confucius about government.

2. Confucius replied, "There is government when the prince is prince, and the minister is minister; when the father is father, and the son is son."

3. "Good!" said the Duke. "If, indeed, the prince be not prince, the minister not minister, the father not father, and the son not son, although I have my revenue, can I enjoy it?"

CHAPTER XII. 1. The Master said, "Ah! It is Yu who could with half a word settle litigations!"

2. Tsze-lu never slept over a promise.

CHAPTER XIII. The Master said, "In hearing litigations, I am like any other body. What is necessary, however, is to cause the people to have no litigations."

CHAPTER XIV. Tsze-chang asked about government. The Master said, "The art of governing is to keep its affairs before the mind without weariness, and to practise them with undeviating consistency."

CHAPTER XV. The Master said, "By extensively studying all learning, and keeping himself under the restraint of the rules of propriety, one may thus likewise not err from what is right."

CHAPTER XVI. The Master said, "The superior man seeks to perfect the admirable qualities of men, and does not seek to perfect their bad qualities. The mean man does the opposite of this."

CHAPTER XVII. Chi K'ang asked Confucius about government. Confucius replied, "To govern means to rectify. If you lead on the people with correctness, who will dare not to be correct?"

CHAPTER XVIII. Chi K'ang, distressed about the number of thieves in the State, inquired of Confucius how to do away with them. Confucius said, "If you, sir, were not covetous, although you should reward them to do it, they would not steal."

CHAPTER XIX. Chi K'ang asked Confucius about government, saying, "What do you say to killing the unprincipled for the good of the principled?" Confucius replied, "Sir, in carrying on your government, why should you use killing at all? Let your evinced desires be for what is good, and the people will be good. The relation between superiors and inferiors is like that between the wind and the grass. The grass must bend when the wind blows across it."

CHAPTER XX. 1. Tsze-chang asked, "What must the officer be who may be said to be distinguished?"

2. The Master said, "What is it you call being distinguished?"

3. Tsze-chang replied, "It is to be heard of through the State, to be heard of throughout his clan."

4. The Master said, "That is notoriety, not distinction.

5. "Now the man of distinction is solid and straightforward, and loves righteousness. He examines people's words, and looks at their countenances. He is anxious to humble himself to others. Such a man will be distinguished in the country; he will be distinguished in his clan.`

6. "As to the man of notoriety, he assumes the appearance of virtue, but his actions are opposed to it, and he rests in this character without any doubts about himself. Such a man will be heard of in the country; he will be heard of in the clan."

CHAPTER XXI. 1. Fan Ch'ih rambling with the Master under the trees about the rain altars, said, "I venture to ask how to exalt virtue, to correct cherished evil, and to discover delusions."

2. The Master said, "Truly a good question!

3. "If doing what is to be done be made the first business, and success a secondary consideration—is not this the way to exalt virtue? To assail one's own wickedness and not assail that of others—is not this the way to correct cherished evil? For a morning's

anger to disregard one's own life, and involve that of his parents— is not this a case of delusion?"

CHAPTER XXII. 1. Fan Ch'ih asked about benevolence. The Master said, "It is to love all men." He asked about knowledge. The Master said, "It is to know all men."

2. Fan Ch'ih did not immediately understand these answers.

3. The Master said, "Employ the upright and put aside all the crooked; in this way the crooked can be made to be upright."

4. Fan Ch'ih retired, and, seeing Tsze-hsia, he said to him, "A little while ago, I had an interview with our Master, and asked him about knowledge. He said, 'Employ the upright and put aside all the crooked; in this way the crooked; will be made to be upright.' What did he mean?"

5. Tsze-hsia said, "Truly rich is his saying!

6. "Shun, being in possession of the kingdom, selected from among all the people and employed Kao-yao, on which all who were devoid of virtue disappeared. T'ang, being in possession of the kingdom, selected from among all the people and employed I Yin, and all who were devoid of virtue disappeared."

CHAPTER XXIII. Tsze-kung asked about friendship. The Master said, "Faithfully admonish your friend, and skilfully lead him on. If you find him impracticable, stop. Do not disgrace yourself."

CHAPTER XXIV. The philosopher Tsang said, "The superior man on grounds of culture meets with his friends, and by their friendship helps his virtue."

Book XIII

TSZE-LU

CHAPTER I. 1. Tsze-lu asked about government. The Master said, "Go before the people with your example, and be laborious in their affairs."

2. He requested further instruction, and was answered, "Be not weary in these things."

CHAPTER II. 1. Chung-kung, being chief minister to the head of the Chi family, asked about government. The Master said, "Employ first the services of your various officers, pardon small faults, and raise to office men of virtue and talents."

2. Chung-kung said, "How shall I know the men of virtue and talent, so that I may raise them to office?" He was answered, "Raise to office those whom you know. As to those whom you do not know, will others neglect them?"

CHAPTER III. 1. Tsze-lu said, "The ruler of Wei has been waiting for you, in order with you to administer the government. What will you consider the first thing to be done?"

2. The Master replied, "What is necessary is to rectify names."

3. "So, indeed!" said Tsze-lu. "You are wide of the mark! Why must there be such rectification?"

4. The Master said, "How uncultivated you are, Yu! A superior man, in regard to what he does not know, shows a cautious reserve.

5. "If names be not correct, language is not in accordance with the truth of things. If language be not in accordance with the truth of things, affairs cannot be carried on to success.

6. "When affairs cannot be carried on to success, proprieties and music will not flourish. When proprieties and music do not flourish, punishments will not be properly awarded. When punishments are not properly awarded, the people do not know how to move hand or foot.

7. "Therefore a superior man considers it necessary that the names he uses may be spoken appropriately, and also that what he speaks may be carried out appropriately. What the superior man requires is just that in his words there may be nothing incorrect."

CHAPTER IV. 1. Fan Ch'ih requested to be taught husbandry. The Master said, "I am not so good for that as an old husbandman." He requested also to be taught gardening, and was answered, "I am not so good for that as an old gardener."

2. Fan Ch'ih having gone out, the Master said, "A small man, indeed, is Fan Hsu!

3. "If a superior man love propriety, the people will not dare not to be reverent. If he love righteousness, the people will not dare

not to submit to his example. If he love good faith, the people will not dare not to be sincere. Now, when these things obtain, the people from all quarters will come to him, bearing their children on their backs; what need has he of a knowledge of husbandry?"

CHAPTER V. The Master said, "Though a man may be able to recite the three hundred odes, yet if, when entrusted with a governmental charge, he knows not how to act, or if, when sent to any quarter on a mission, he cannot give his replies unassisted, notwithstanding the extent of his learning, of what practical use is it?"

CHAPTER VI. The Master said, "When a prince's personal conduct is correct, his government is effective without the issuing of orders. If his personal conduct is not correct, he may issue orders, but they will not be followed."

CHAPTER VII. The Master said, "The governments of Lu and Wei are brothers."

CHAPTER VIII. The Master said of Ching, a scion of the ducal family of Wei, that he knew the economy of a family well. When he began to have means, he said, "Ha! Here is a collection!" When they were a little increased, he said, "Ha! This is complete!" When he had become rich, he said, "Ha! This is admirable!"

CHAPTER IX. 1. When the Master went to Wei, Zan Yu acted as driver of his carriage.

2. The Master observed, "How numerous are the people!"

3. Yu said, "Since they are thus numerous, what more shall be done for them?" "Enrich them," was the reply.

4. "And when they have been enriched, what more shall be done?" The Master said, "Teach them."

CHAPTER X. The Master said, "If there were any of the princes who would employ me, in the course of twelve months I should have done something considerable. In three years, the government would be perfected."

CHAPTER XI. The Master said, " 'If good men were to govern a country in succession for a hundred years, they would be able to transform the violently bad, and dispense with capital punishments.' True indeed is this saying!"

CHAPTER XII. The Master said, "If a truly royal ruler were to arise, it would still require a generation, and then virtue would prevail."

CHAPTER XIII. The Master said, "If a minister make his own conduct correct, what difficulty will he have in assisting in government? If he cannot rectify himself, what has he to do with rectifying others?"

CHAPTER XIV. The disciple Zan returning from the court, the Master said to him, "How are you so late?" He replied, "We had government business." The Master said, "It must have been family affairs. If there had been government business, though I am not now in office, I should have been consulted about it."

CHAPTER XV. 1. The Duke Ting asked whether there was a single sentence which could make a country prosperous. Confucius replied, "Such an effect cannot be expected from one sentence.

2. "There is a saying, however, which people have: 'To be a prince is difficult; to be a minister is not easy.'

3. "If a ruler knows this—the difficulty of being a prince—may there not be expected from this one sentence the prosperity of his country?"

4. The Duke then said, "Is there a single sentence which can ruin a country?" Confucius replied, "Such an effect as that cannot be expected from one sentence. There is, however, the saying which people have: 'I have no pleasure in being a prince, but only in that no one can offer any opposition to what I say!'

5. "If a ruler's words be good, is it not also good that no one oppose them? But if they are not good, and no one opposes them, may there not be expected from this one sentence the ruin of his country?"

CHAPTER XVI. 1. The Duke of Sheh asked about government.

2. The Master said, "Good government obtains when those who are near are made happy, and those who are far off are attracted."

CHAPTER XVII. Tsze-hsia, being governor of Chu-fu, asked about government. The Master said, "Do not be desirous to have things done quickly; do not look at small advantages. Desire to have things done quickly prevents their being done thoroughly. Looking at small advantages prevents great affairs from being accomplished."

CHAPTER XVIII. 1. The Duke of Sheh informed Confucius, saying, "Among us here there are those who may be styled upright in their conduct. If their father have stolen a sheep, they will bear witness to the fact."

2. Confucius said, "Among us, in our part of the country, those who are upright are different from this. The father conceals the

misconduct of the son, and the son conceals the misconduct of the father. Uprightness is to be found in this."

CHAPTER XIX. Fan Ch'ih asked about perfect virtue. The Master said, "It is, in retirement, to be sedately grave; in the management of business, to be reverently attentive; in intercourse with others, to be strictly sincere. Though a man go among rude, uncultivated tribes, these qualities may not be neglected."

CHAPTER XX. 1. Tsze-kung asked, saying, "What qualities must a man possess to entitle him to be called an officer?" The Master said, "He who in his conduct of himself maintains a sense of shame, and when sent to any quarter will not disgrace his prince's commission, deserves to be called an officer."

2. Tsze-kung pursued, "I venture to ask who may be placed in the next-lower rank?" And he was told, "He whom the circle of his relatives pronounce to be filial, whom his fellow-villagers and neighbors pronounce to be fraternal."

3. Again the disciple asked, "I venture to ask about the class still next in order." The Master said, "They are determined to be sincere in what they say, and to carry out what they do. They are obstinate little men. Yet perhaps they may make the next class."

4. Tsze-kung finally inquired, "Of what sort are those of the present day who engage in government?" The Master said "Pooh! They are so many pecks and hampers, not worth being taken into account."

CHAPTER XXI. The Master said, "Since I cannot get men pursuing the due medium, to whom I might communicate my instructions, I must find the ardent and the cautiously decided. The ardent will advance and lay hold of truth; the cautiously decided will keep themselves from what is wrong."

CHAPTER XXII. 1. The Master said, "The people of the south have a saying: 'A man without constancy cannot be either a wizard or a doctor.' Good!

2. "Inconstant in his virtue, he will be visited with disgrace."

3. The Master said, "This arises simply from not attending to the prognostication."

CHAPTER XXIII. The Master said, "The superior man is affable, but not adulatory; the mean man is adulatory, but not affable."

CHAPTER XXIV. Tsze-kung asked, saying, "What do you say of a man who is loved by all the people of his neighborhood?" The Master replied, "We may not for that accord our approval of him." "And what do you say of him who is hated by all the people of his neighborhood?" The Master said, "We may not for that conclude that he is bad. It is better than either of these cases that the good in the neighborhood love him, and the bad hate him."

CHAPTER XXV. The Master said, "The superior man is easy to serve and difficult to please. If you try to please him in any way which is not accordant with right, he will not be pleased. But in his employment of men, he uses them according to their capacity. The mean man is difficult to serve, and easy to please. If you try to please him, though it be in a way which is not accordant with right, he may be pleased. But in his employment of men, he wishes them to be equal to everything."

CHAPTER XXVI. The Master said, "The superior man has a dignified ease without pride. The mean man has pride without a dignified ease."

CHAPTER XXVII. The Master said, "The firm, the enduring, the simple, and the modest are near to virtue."

CHAPTER XXVIII. Tsze-lu asked, saying, "What qualities must a man possess to entitle him to be called a scholar?" The Master said, "He must be thus—earnest, urgent, and bland: among his friends, earnest and urgent; among his brethren, bland."

CHAPTER XXIX. The Master said, "Let a good man teach the people seven years, and they may then likewise be employed in war."

CHAPTER XXX. The Master said, "To lead an uninstructed people to war is to throw them away."

Book XIV

HSIEN WAN

CHAPTER I. Hsien asked what was shameful. The Master said, "When good government prevails in a State, to be thinking only of salary; and, when bad government prevails, to be thinking, in the same way, only of salary—this is shameful."

CHAPTER II. 1. "When the love of superiority, boasting, resentments, and covetousness are repressed, this may be deemed perfect virtue."

2. The Master said, "This may be regarded as the achievement of what is difficult. But I do not know that it is to be deemed perfect virtue."

CHAPTER III. The Master said, "The scholar who cherishes the love of comfort is not fit to be deemed a scholar."

CHAPTER IV. The Master said, "When good government prevails in a State, language may be lofty and bold, and actions the same. When bad government prevails, the actions may be lofty and bold, but the language may be with some reserve."

CHAPTER V. The Master said, "The virtuous will be sure to speak correctly, but those whose speech is good may not always be virtuous. Men of principle are sure to be bold, but those who are bold may not always be men of principle."

CHAPTER VI. Nan-kung Kwo, submitting an inquiry to Confucius, said, "I was skilful at archery, and Ao could move a boat along upon the land, but neither of them died a natural death. Yu and Chi personally wrought at the toils of husbandry, and they became possessors of the kingdom." The Master made no reply; but when Nan-kung Kwo went out, he said, "A superior man indeed is this! An esteemer of virtue indeed is this!"

CHAPTER VII. The Master said, "Superior men, and yet not always virtuous, there have been, alas! But there never has been a mean man and, at the same time, virtuous."

CHAPTER VIII. The Master said, "Can there be love which does not lead to strictness with its object? Can there be loyalty which does not lead to the instruction of its object?"

CHAPTER IX. The Master said, "In preparing the governmental notifications, P'i Shan first made the rough draft; Shi-shu examined and discussed its contents; Tsze-yu, the manager of foreign intercourse, then polished the style; and, finally, Tsze-ch'an of Tung-li gave it the proper elegance and finish."

CHAPTER X. 1. Someone asked about Tsze-ch'an. The Master said, "He was a kind man."

2. He asked about Tsze-hsi. The Master said, "That man! That man!"

3. He asked about Kwan Chung. "For him," said the Master, "the city of Pien, with three hundred families, was taken from the chief of the Po family, who did not utter a murmuring word, though, to the end of his life, he had only coarse rice to eat."

CHAPTER XI. The Master said, "To be poor without murmuring is difficult. To be rich without being proud is easy."

CHAPTER XII. The Master said, "Mang Kung-ch'o is more than fit to be chief officer in the families of Chao and Wei, but he is not fit to be great officer to either of the States Tang or Hsieh."

CHAPTER XIII. 1. Tsze-lu asked what constituted a COMPLETE man. The Master said, "Suppose a man with the knowledge of Tsang Wu-chung, the freedom from covetousness of Kung-ch'o, the bravery of Chwang of Pien, and the varied talents of Zan Ch'iu; add to these the accomplishments of the rules of propriety and music: such a one might be reckoned a COMPLETE man."

2. He then added, "But what is the necessity for a complete man of the present day to have all these things? The man who, in the view of gain, thinks of righteousness; who in the view of danger is prepared to give up his life; and who does not forget an old agreement however far back it extends: such a man may be reckoned a COMPLETE man."

CHAPTER XIV. 1. The Master asked Kung-ming Chia about Kung-shu Wan, saying, "Is it true that your master speaks not, laughs not, and takes not?"

2. Kung-ming Chia replied, "This has arisen from the reporters going beyond the truth. My master speaks when it is the time to

speak, and so men do not get tired of his speaking. He laughs when there is occasion to be joyful, and so men do not get tired of his laughing. He takes when it is consistent with righteousness to do so, and so men do not get tired of his taking." The Master said, "So! But is it so with him?"

CHAPTER XV. The Master said, "Tsang Wu-chung, keeping possession of Fang, asked of the Duke of Lu to appoint a successor to him in his family. Although it may be said that he was not using force with his sovereign, I believe he was."

CHAPTER XVI. The Master said, "The Duke Wan of Tsin was crafty and not upright. The Duke Hwan of Ch'i was upright and not crafty."

CHAPTER XVII. 1. Tsze-lu said, "The Duke Hwan caused his brother Chiu to be killed, when Shao Hu died with his master, but Kwan Chung did not die. May not I say that he was wanting in virtue?"

2. The Master said, "The Duke Hwan assembled all the princes together, and that not with weapons of war and chariots: it was all through the influence of Kwan Chung. Whose beneficence was like his? Whose beneficence was like his?"

CHAPTER XVIII. 1. Tsze-kung said, "Kwan Chung, I apprehend, was wanting in virtue. When the Duke Hwan caused his brother Chiu to be killed, Kwan Chung was not able to die with him. Moreover, he became prime minister to Hwan."

2. The Master said, "Kwan Chung acted as prime minister to the Duke Hwan, made him leader of all the princes, and united and rectified the whole kingdom. Down to the present day, the people

enjoy the gifts which he conferred. But for Kwan Chung, we should now be wearing our hair unbound, and the lappets of our coats buttoning on the left side.

3. "Will you require from him the small fidelity of common men and common women, who would commit suicide in a stream or ditch, no one knowing anything about them?"

CHAPTER XIX. 1. The great officer, Hsien, who had been family-minister to Kung-shu Wan, ascended to the prince's court in company with Wan.

2. The Master, having heard of it, said, "He deserved to be considered WAN (the accomplished)."

CHAPTER XX. 1. The Master was speaking about the unprincipled course of the Duke Ling of Wei, when Ch'i K'ang said, "Since he is of such a character, how is it he does not lose his State?"

2. Confucius said, "The Chung-shu Yu has the superintendence of his guests and of strangers; the litanist, T'o, has the management of his ancestral temple; and Wang-sun Chia has the direction of the army and forces: with such officers as these, how should he lose his State?"

CHAPTER XXI. The Master said, "He who speaks without modesty will find it difficult to make his words good."

CHAPTER XXII. 1. Chan Ch'ang murdered the Duke Chien of Ch'i.

2. Confucius bathed, went to court, and informed the Duke Ai, saying, "Chan Hang has slain his sovereign. I beg that you will undertake to punish him."

3. The Duke said, "Inform the chiefs of the three families of it."

4. Confucius retired, and said, "Following in the rear of the great officers, I did not dare not to represent such a matter, and my prince says, 'Inform the chiefs of the three families of it.'"

5. He went to the chiefs, and informed them, but they would not act. Confucius then said, "Following in the rear of the great officers, I did not dare not to represent such a matter."

CHAPTER XXIII. Tsze-lu asked how a ruler should be served. The Master said, "Do not impose on him, and, moreover, withstand him to his face."

CHAPTER XXIV. The Master said, "The progress of the superior man is upwards; the progress of the mean man is downwards."

CHAPTER XXV. The Master said, "In ancient times, men learned with a view to their own improvement. Nowadays, men learn with a view to the approbation of others."

CHAPTER XXVI. 1. Chu Po-yu sent a messenger with friendly inquiries to Confucius.

2. Confucius sat with him, and questioned him. "What," said he, "is your master engaged in?" The messenger replied, "My master is anxious to make his faults few, but he has not yet succeeded." He then went out, and the Master said, "A messenger indeed! A messenger indeed!"

CHAPTER XXVII. The Master said, "He who is not in any particular office has nothing to do with plans for the administration of its duties."

CHAPTER XXVIII. The philosopher Tsang said, "The superior man, in his thoughts, does not go out of his place."

CHAPTER XXIX. The Master said, "The superior man is modest in his speech, but exceeds in his actions."

CHAPTER XXX. 1. The Master said, "The way of the superior man is threefold, but I am not equal to it. Virtuous, he is free from anxieties; wise, he is free from perplexities; bold, he is free from fear."

2. Tsze-kung said, "Master, that is what you yourself say."

CHAPTER XXXI. Tsze-kung was in the habit of comparing men together. The Master said, "Tsze must have reached a high pitch of excellence! Now, I have not leisure for this."

CHAPTER XXXII. The Master said, "I will not be concerned at men's not knowing me; I will be concerned at my own want of ability."

CHAPTER XXXIII. The Master said, "He who does not anticipate attempts to deceive him, nor think beforehand of his not being believed, and yet apprehends these things readily when they occur—is he not a man of superior worth?"

CHAPTER XXXIV. 1. Wei-shang Mau said to Confucius, "Ch'iu, how is it that you keep roosting about? Is it not that you are an insinuating talker?"

2. Confucius said, "I do not dare to play the part of such a talker, but I hate obstinacy."

CHAPTER XXXV. The Master said, "A horse is called a ch'i, not because of its strength, but because of its other good qualities."

CHAPTER XXXVI. 1. Someone said, "What do you say concerning the principle that injury should be recompensed with kindness?"

2. The Master said, "With what then will you recompense kindness?

3. "Recompense injury with justice, and recompense kindness with kindness."

CHAPTER XXXVII. 1. The Master said, "Alas! There is no one that knows me."

2. Tsze-kung said, "What do you mean by thus saying that no one knows you?" The Master replied, "I do not murmur against Heaven. I do not grumble against men. My studies lie low, and my penetration rises high. But there is Heaven—that knows me!"

CHAPTER XXXVIII. 1. The Kung-po Liao, having slandered Tsze-lu to Chi-sun, Tsze-fu Ching-po informed Confucius of it, saying, "Our master is certainly being led astray by the Kung-po Liao, but I have still power enough left to cut Liao off, and expose his corpse in the market and in the court."

2. The Master said, "If my principles are to advance, it is so ordered. If they are to fall to the ground, it is so ordered. What can the Kung-po Liao do where such ordering is concerned?"

CHAPTER XXXIX. 1. The Master said, "Some men of worth retire from the world.

2. "Some retire from particular States.

3. "Some retire because of disrespectful looks.

4. "Some retire because of contradictory language."

CHAPTER XL. The Master said, "Those who have done this are seven men."

CHAPTER XLI. Tsze-lu happening to pass the night in Shih-man, the gatekeeper said to him, "Whom do you come from?"

Tsze-lu said, "From Mr. K'ung." "It is he, is it not," said the other, "who knows the impracticable nature of the times and yet will be doing in them."

CHAPTER XLII. 1. The Master was playing, one day, on a musical stone in Wei, when a man, carrying a straw basket, passed the door of the house where Confucius was, and said, "His heart is full who so beats the musical stone."

2. A little while after, he added, "How contemptible is the one-ideaed obstinacy those sounds display! When one is taken no notice of, he has simply at once to give over his wish for public employment. 'Deep water must be crossed with the clothes on; shallow water may be crossed with the clothes held up.' "

3. The Master said, "How determined is he in his purpose! But this is not difficult!"

CHAPTER XLIII. 1. Tsze-chang said, "What is meant when the Shu says that Kao-tsung, while observing the usual imperial mourning, was for three years without speaking?"

2. The Master said, "Why must Kao-tsung be referred to as an example of this? The ancients all did so. When the sovereign died, the officers all attended to their several duties, taking instructions from the prime minister for three years."

CHAPTER XLIV. The Master said, "When rulers love to observe the rules of propriety, the people respond readily to the calls on them for service."

CHAPTER XLV. Tsze-lu asked what constituted the superior man. The Master said, "The cultivation of himself in reverential carefulness." "And is this all?" said Tsze-lu. "He cultivates himself so as to give rest to others," was the reply. "And is this all?" again asked Tsze-lu. The Master said, "He cultivates himself so as to give rest to all the people. He cultivates himself so as to give rest to all the people—even Yao and Shun were still solicitous about this."

CHAPTER XLVI. Yuan Zang was squatting on his heels, and so waited the approach of the Master, who said to him, "In youth not humble as befits a junior; in manhood, doing nothing worthy of being handed down; and living on to old age: this is to be a pest." With this he hit him on the shank with his staff.

CHAPTER XLVI. 1. A youth of the village of Ch'ueh was employed by Confucius to carry the messages between him and his visitors. Someone asked about him, saying, "I suppose he has made great progress."

2. The Master said, "I observe that he is fond of occupying the seat of a full-grown man; I observe that he walks shoulder to shoulder with his elders. He is not one who is seeking to make progress in learning. He wishes quickly to become a man."

Book XV

WEI LING KUNG

CHAPTER I. 1. The Duke Ling of Wei asked Confucius about tactics. Confucius replied, "I have heard all about sacrificial vessels, but I have not learned military matters." On this, he took his departure the next day.

2. When he was in Chan, their provisions were exhausted, and his followers became so ill that they were unable to rise.

3. Tsze-lu, with evident dissatisfaction, said, "Has the superior man likewise to endure in this way?" The Master said, "The superior man may indeed have to endure want, but the mean man, when he is in want, gives way to unbridled license."

CHAPTER II. 1. The Master said, "Ts'ze, you think, I suppose, that I am one who learns many things and keeps them in memory?"

2. Tsze-kung replied, "Yes—but perhaps it is not so?"

3. "No," was the answer; "I seek a unity all-pervading."

CHAPTER III. The Master said, "Yu, those who know virtue are few."

CHAPTER IV. The Master said, "May not Shun be instanced as having governed efficiently without exertion? What did he do? He did nothing but gravely and reverently occupy his royal seat."

CHAPTER V. 1. Tsze-chang asked how a man should conduct himself so as to be everywhere appreciated.

2. The Master said, "Let his words be sincere and truthful, and his actions honourable and careful; such conduct may be practised among the rude tribes of the South or the North. If his words be not sincere and truthful and his actions not honourable and careful, will he, with such conduct, be appreciated, even in his neighborhood?

3. "When he is standing, let him see those two things, as it were, fronting him. When he is in a carriage, let him see them attached to the yoke. Then may he subsequently carry them into practice."

4. Tsze-chang wrote these counsels on the end of his sash.

CHAPTER VI. 1. The Master said, "Truly straightforward was the historiographer Yu. When good government prevailed in his State, he was like an arrow. When bad government prevailed, he was like an arrow.

2. A superior man indeed is Chu Po-yu! When good government prevails in his State, he is to be found in office. When bad government prevails, he can roll his principles up, and keep them in his breast."

CHAPTER VII. The Master said, "When a man may be spoken with, not to speak to him is to err in reference to the man. When a man may not be spoken with, to speak to him is to err in reference to our words. The wise err neither in regard to their man nor to their words."

CHAPTER VIII. The Master said, "The determined scholar and the man of virtue will not seek to live at the expense of injuring their virtue. They will even sacrifice their lives to preserve their virtue complete."

CHAPTER IX. Tsze-kung asked about the practice of virtue. The Master said, "The mechanic, who wishes to do his work well must first sharpen his tools. When you are living in any State take service with the most worthy among its great officers, and make friends of the most virtuous among its scholars."

CHAPTER X. 1. Yen Yuan asked how the government of a country should be administered.

2. The Master said, "Follow the seasons of Hsia.

3. "Ride in the state carriage of Yin.

4. "Wear the ceremonial cap of Chau.

5. "Let the music be the Shao with its pantomimes.

6. "Banish the songs of Chang, and keep far from specious talkers. The songs of Chang are licentious; specious talkers are dangerous."

CHAPTER XI. The Master said, "If a man take no thought about what is distant, he will find sorrow near at hand."

CHAPTER XII. The Master said, "It is all over! I have not seen one who loves virtue as he loves beauty."

CHAPTER XIII. The Master said, "Was not Tsang Wan like one who had stolen his situation? He knew the virtue and the talents of Hui of Liu-hsia, and yet did not procure that he should stand with him in court."

CHAPTER XIV. The Master said, "He who requires much from himself and little from others will keep himself from being the object of resentment."

CHAPTER XV. The Master said, "When a man is not in the habit of saying 'What shall I think of this? What shall I think of this?' I can indeed do nothing with him!"

CHAPTER XVI. The Master said, "When a number of people are together, for a whole day, without their conversation turning on righteousness, and when they are fond of carrying out the suggestions of a small shrewdness—theirs is indeed a hard case."

CHAPTER XVII. The Master said, "The superior man in everything considers righteousness to be essential. He performs it according to the rules of propriety. He brings it forth in humility. He completes it with sincerity. This is indeed a superior man."

CHAPTER XVIII. The Master said, "The superior man is distressed by his want of ability. He is not distressed by men's not knowing him."

CHAPTER XIX. The Master said, "The superior man dislikes the thought of his name not being mentioned after his death."

CHAPTER XX. The Master said, "What the superior man seeks is in himself. What the mean man seeks is in others."

CHAPTER XXI. The Master said, "The superior man is dignified, but does not wrangle. He is sociable, but not a partisan."

CHAPTER XXII. The Master said, "The superior man does not promote a man simply on account of his words, nor does he put aside good words because of the man."

CHAPTER XXIII. Tsze-kung asked, saying, "Is there one word which may serve as a rule of practice for all one's life?" The Master said, "Is not RECIPROCITY such a word? What you do not want done to yourself, do not do to others."

CHAPTER XXIV. 1. The Master said, "In my dealings with men, whose evil do I blame, whose goodness do I praise, beyond what is proper? If I do sometimes exceed in praise, there must be ground for it in my examination of the individual.

2. "This people supplied the ground why the three dynasties pursued the path of straightforwardness."

CHAPTER XXV. The Master said, "Even in my early days, a historiographer would leave a blank in his text, and he who had a horse would lend him to another to ride. Now, alas! There are no such things."

CHAPTER XXVI. The Master said, "Specious words confound virtue. Want of forbearance in small matters confounds great plans."

CHAPTER XXVII. The Master said, "When the multitude hate a man, it is necessary to examine into the case. When the multitude like a man, it is necessary to examine into the case."

CHAPTER XXVIII. The Master said, "A man can enlarge the principles which he follows; those principles do not enlarge the man."

CHAPTER XXIX. The Master said, "To have faults and not to reform them—this, indeed, should be pronounced having faults."

CHAPTER XXX. The Master said, "I have been the whole day without eating, and the whole night without sleeping—occupied with thinking. It was of no use. The better plan is to learn."

CHAPTER XXXI. The Master said, "The object of the superior man is truth. Food is not his object. There is plowing; even in that there is sometimes want. So with learning; emolument may be found in it. The superior man is anxious lest he should not get truth; he is not anxious lest poverty should come upon him."

CHAPTER XXXII. 1. The Master said, "When a man's knowledge is sufficient to attain, and his virtue is not sufficient to enable him to hold, whatever he may have gained he will lose again.

2. "When his knowledge is sufficient to attain, and he has virtue enough to hold fast, if he cannot govern with dignity, the people will not respect him.

3. "When his knowledge is sufficient to attain, and he has virtue enough to hold fast; when he governs also with dignity, yet if he try to move the people contrary to the rules of propriety: full excellence is not reached."

CHAPTER XXXIII. The Master said, "The superior man cannot be known in little matters; but he may be entrusted with great concerns. The small man may not be entrusted with great concerns, but he may be known in little matters."

CHAPTER XXXIV. The Master said, "Virtue is more to man than either water or fire. I have seen men die from treading on water and fire, but I have never seen a man die from treading the course of virtue."

CHAPTER XXXV. The Master said, "Let every man consider virtue as what devolves on himself. He may not yield the performance of it even to his teacher."

CHAPTER XXXVI. The Master said, "The superior man is correctly firm, and not firm merely."

CHAPTER XXXVII. The Master said, "A minister, in serving his prince, reverently discharges his duties, and makes his emolument a secondary consideration."

CHAPTER XXXVIII. The Master said, "In teaching there should be no distinction of classes."

CHAPTER XXXIX. The Master said, "Those whose courses are different cannot lay plans for one another."

CHAPTER XL. The Master said, "In language it is simply required that it convey the meaning."

CHAPTER XLI. 1. The music-master, Mien, having called upon him, when they came to the steps, the Master said, "Here are the steps." When they came to the mat for the guest to sit upon, he said, "Here is the mat." When all were seated, the Master informed him, saying, "So and so is here; so and so is here."

2. The music-master, Mien, having gone out, Tsze-chang asked, saying "Is it the rule to tell those things to the music-master?"

3. The Master said, "Yes. This is certainly the rule for those who lead the blind."

Book XVI

KE SHE

CHAPTER I. 1. The head of the Chi family was going to attack Chwan-yu.

2. Zan Yu and Chi-lu had an interview with Confucius, and said, "Our chief, Chi, is going to commence operations against Chwan-yu."

3. Confucius said, "Ch'iu, is it not you who are in fault here?

4. "Now, in regard to Chwan-yu, long ago a former king appointed its ruler to preside over the sacrifices to the eastern Mang; moreover, it is in the midst of the territory of our State; and its ruler is a minister in direct connection with the sovereign: what has your chief to do with attacking it?"

5. Zan Yu said, "Our master wishes the thing; neither of us two ministers wishes it."

6. Confucius said, "Ch'iu, there are the words of Chau Zan, 'When he can put forth his ability, he takes his place in the ranks

of office; when he finds himself unable to do so, he retires from it. How can he be used as a guide to a blind man who does not support him when tottering, nor raise him up when fallen?'

7. "And further, you speak wrongly. When a tiger or rhinoceros escapes from his cage; when a tortoise or piece of jade is injured in its repository: whose is the fault?"

8. Zan Yu said, "But at present, Chwan-yu is strong and near to Pi; if our chief do not now take it, it will hereafter be a sorrow to his descendants."

9. Confucius said "Ch'iu, the superior man hates those declining to say 'I want such and such a thing' and framing explanations for the conduct.

10. "I have heard that rulers of States and chiefs of families are not troubled lest their people should be few, but are troubled lest they should not keep their several places; that they are not troubled with fears of poverty, but are troubled with fears of a want of contented repose among the people in their several places. For when the people keep their several places, there will be no poverty; when harmony prevails, there will be no scarcity of people; and when there is such a contented repose, there will be no rebellious upsettings.

11. "So it is. Therefore, if remoter people are not submissive, all the influences of civil culture and virtue are to be cultivated to attract them to be so; and when they have been so attracted, they must be made contented and tranquil.

12. "Now, here are you, Yu and Ch'iu, assisting your chief. Remoter people are not submissive, and, with your help, he

cannot attract them to him. In his own territory there are divisions and downfalls, leavings and separations, and, with your help, he cannot preserve it.

13. "And yet he is planning these hostile movements within the State. I am afraid that the sorrow of the Chi-sun family will not be on account of Chwan-yu, but will be found within the screen of their own court."

CHAPTER II. 1. Confucius said, "When good government prevails in the empire, ceremonies, music, and punitive military expeditions proceed from the son of Heaven. When bad government prevails in the empire, ceremonies, music, and punitive military expeditions proceed from the princes. When these things proceed from the great officers of the princes, as a rule, the cases will be few in which they do not lose their power in ten generations. When they proceed from the great officers of the princes, as a rule, the cases will be few in which they do not lose their power in five generations. When the subsidiary ministers of the great officers hold in their grasp the orders of the State, as a rule, the cases will be few in which they do not lose their power in three generations.

2. "When right principles prevail in the kingdom, government will not be in the hands of the great officers.

3. "When right principles prevail in the kingdom, there will be no discussions among the common people."

CHAPTER III. Confucius said, "The revenue of the State has left the ducal house now for five generations. The government has been in the hands of the great officers for four generations.

On this account, the descendants of the three Hwan are much reduced."

CHAPTER IV. Confucius said, "There are three friendships which are advantageous, and three which are injurious. Friendship with the upright; friendship with the sincere; and friendship with the man of much observation: these are advantageous. Friendship with the man of specious airs; friendship with the insinuatingly soft; and friendship with the glib-tongued: these are injurious."

CHAPTER V. Confucius said, "There are three things men find enjoyment in which are advantageous, and three things they find enjoyment in which are injurious. To find enjoyment in the discriminating study of ceremonies and music; to find enjoyment in speaking of the goodness of others; to find enjoyment in having many worthy friends: these are advantageous. To find enjoyment in extravagant pleasures; to find enjoyment in idleness and sauntering; to find enjoyment in the pleasures of feasting: these are injurious."

CHAPTER VI. Confucius said, "There are three errors to which they who stand in the presence of a man of virtue and station are liable. They may speak when it does not come to them to speak; this is called rashness. They may not speak when it comes to them to speak; this is called concealment. They may speak without looking at the countenance of their superior; this is called blindness."

CHAPTER VII. Confucius said, "There are three things which the superior man guards against. In youth, when the physical powers are not yet settled, he guards against lust. When he is strong and the physical powers are full of vigour, he guards against quarrelsomeness. When he is old, and the animal powers are decayed, he guards against covetousness."

CHAPTER VIII. 1. Confucius said, "There are three things of which the superior man stands in awe. He stands in awe of the ordinances of Heaven. He stands in awe of great men. He stands in awe of the words of sages.

2. "The mean man does not know the ordinances of Heaven, and consequently does not stand in awe of them. He is disrespectful to great men. He makes sport of the words of sages."

CHAPTER IX. Confucius said, "Those who are born with the possession of knowledge are the highest class of men. Those who learn, and so, readily, get possession of knowledge, are the next. Those who are dull and stupid, and yet compass the learning, are another class next to these. As to those who are dull and stupid and yet do not learn—they are the lowest of the people."

CHAPTER X. Confucius said, "The superior man has nine things which are subjects with him of thoughtful consideration. In regard to the use of his eyes, he is anxious to see clearly. In regard to the use of his ears, he is anxious to hear distinctly. In regard to his countenance, he is anxious that it should be benign. In regard to his demeanor, he is anxious that it should be respectful. In regard to his speech, he is anxious that it should be sincere. In regard to his doing of business, he is anxious that it should be reverently careful. In regard to what he doubts about, he is anxious to question others. When he is angry, he thinks of the difficulties his anger may involve him in. When he sees gain to be got, he thinks of righteousness."

CHAPTER XI. 1. Confucius said, "Contemplating good, and pursuing it, as if they could not reach it; contemplating evil, and shrinking from it, as they would from thrusting the hand into boiling water: I have seen such men, as I have heard such words.

2. "Living in retirement to study their aims, and practising righteousness to carry out their principles: I have heard these words, but I have not seen such men."

CHAPTER XII. 1. The Duke Ching of Ch'i had a thousand teams, each of four horses, but on the day of his death, the people did not praise him for a single virtue. Po-i and Shu-ch'i died of hunger at the foot of the Shau-yang mountain, and the people, down to the present time, praise them.

2. "Is not that saying illustrated by this?"

CHAPTER XIII. 1. Ch'an K'ang asked Po-yu, saying, "Have you heard any lessons from your father different from what we have all heard?"

2. Po-yu replied, "No. He was standing alone once, when I passed below the hall with hasty steps, and said to me, 'Have you learned the Odes?' On my replying 'Not yet,' he added, 'If you do not learn the Odes, you will not be fit to converse with.' I retired and studied the Odes.

3. "Another day, he was in the same way standing alone, when I passed by below the hall with hasty steps, and said to me, 'Have you learned the rules of Propriety?' On my replying 'Not yet,' he added, 'If you do not learn the rules of Propriety, your character cannot be established.' I then retired, and learned the rules of Propriety.

4. "I have heard only these two things from him."

5. Ch'ang K'ang retired, and, quite delighted, said, "I asked one thing, and I have got three things. I have heard about the Odes. I have heard about the rules of Propriety. I have also heard that the superior man maintains a distant reserve towards his son."

CHAPTER XIV. The wife of the prince of a State is called by him FU ZAN. She calls herself HSIAO T'UNG. The people of the State call her CHUN FU ZAN, and, to the people of other States, they call her K'WA HSIAO CHUN. The people of other States also call her CHUN FU ZAN.

Book XVII

YANG HO

CHAPTER I. 1. Yang Ho wished to see Confucius, but Confucius would not go to see him. On this, he sent a present of a pig to Confucius, who, having chosen a time when Ho was not at home, went to pay his respects for the gift. He met him, however, on the way.

2. Ho said to Confucius, "Come, let me speak with you." He then asked, "Can he be called benevolent who keeps his jewel in his bosom, and leaves his country to confusion?" Confucius replied, "No." "Can he be called wise who is anxious to be engaged in public employment, and yet is constantly losing the opportunity of being so?" Confucius again said, "No." "The days and months are passing away; the years do not wait for us." Confucius said, "Right; I will go into office."

CHAPTER II. The Master said, "By nature, men are nearly alike; by practice, they get to be wide apart."

CHAPTER III. The Master said, "There are only the wise of the highest class, and the stupid of the lowest class, who cannot be changed."

CHAPTER IV. 1. The Master, having come to Wu-ch'ang, heard there the sound of stringed instruments and singing.

2. Well pleased and smiling, he said, "Why use an ox knife to kill a fowl?"

3. Tsze-yu replied, "Formerly, Master, I heard you say, 'When the man of high station is well instructed, he loves men; when the man of low station is well instructed, he is easily ruled.' "

4. The Master said, "My disciples, Yen's words are right. What I said was only in sport."

CHAPTER V. Kung-shan Fu-zao, when he was holding Pi, and in an attitude of rebellion, invited the Master to visit him, who was rather inclined to go.

2. Tsze-lu was displeased, and said, "Indeed, you cannot go! Why must you think of going to see Kung-shan?"

3. The Master said, "Can it be without some reason that he has invited ME? If anyone employ me, may I not make an eastern Chau?"

CHAPTER VI. Tsze-chang asked Confucius about perfect virtue. Confucius said, "To be able to practise five things everywhere under Heaven constitutes perfect virtue." He begged to ask what they were, and was told, "Gravity, generosity of soul, sincerity, earnestness, and kindness. If you are grave, you will not be treated with disrespect. If you are generous, you will win all. If you are sincere, people will repose trust in you. If you are earnest, you will accomplish much. If you are kind, this will enable you to employ the services of others."

CHAPTER VII. 1. Pi Hsi inviting him to visit him, the Master was inclined to go.

2. Tsze-lu said, "Master, formerly I have heard you say, 'When a man in his own person is guilty of doing evil, a superior man will not associate with him.' Pi Hsi is in rebellion, holding possession of Chung-mau; if you go to him, what shall be said?"

3. The Master said, "Yes, I did use these words. But is it not said that if a thing be really hard, it may be ground without being made thin? Is it not said that if a thing be really white, it may be steeped in a dark fluid without being made black?

4. "Am I a bitter gourd! How can I be hung up out of the way of being eaten?"

CHAPTER VIII. 1. The Master said, "Yu, have you heard the six words to which are attached six becloudings?" Yu replied, "I have not."

2. "Sit down, and I will tell them to you.

3. "There is the love of being benevolent without the love of learning; the beclouding here leads to a foolish simplicity. There is the love of knowing without the love of learning; the beclouding here leads to dissipation of mind. There is the love of being sincere without the love of learning; the beclouding here leads to an injurious disregard of consequences. There is the love of straightforwardness without the love of learning; the beclouding here leads to rudeness. There is the love of boldness

without the love of learning; the beclouding here leads to insubordination. There is the love of firmness without the love of learning; the beclouding here leads to extravagant conduct."

CHAPTER IX. 1. The Master said, "My children, why do you not study the 'Book of Poetry'?

2. "The Odes serve to stimulate the mind.

3. "They may be used for purposes of self-contemplation.

4. "They teach the art of sociability.

5. "They show how to regulate feelings of resentment.

6. "From them you learn the more immediate duty of serving one's father, and the remoter one of serving one's prince.

7. "From them we become largely acquainted with the names of birds, beasts, and plants."

CHAPTER X. The Master said to Po-yu, "Do you give yourself to the Chau-nan and the Shao-nan. The man who has not studied the Chau-nan and the Shao-nan is like one who stands with his face right against a wall. Is he not so?"

CHAPTER XI. The Master said, " 'It is according to the rules of propriety' they say. 'It is according to the rules of propriety,' they say. Are gems and silk all that is meant by propriety? 'It is music,' they say, 'It is music,' they say. Are bells and drums all that is meant by music?"

CHAPTER XII. The Master said, "He who puts on an appearance of stern firmness, while inwardly he is weak, is like one of the small, mean people—yea, is he not like the thief who breaks through, or climbs over, a wall?"

CHAPTER XIII. The Master said, "Your good, careful people of the villages are the thieves of virtue."

CHAPTER XIV. The Master said, "To tell, as we go along, what we have heard on the way is to cast away our virtue."

CHAPTER XV. 1. The Master said, "There are those mean creatures! How impossible it is along with them to serve one's prince!

2. "While they have not got their aims, their anxiety is how to get them. When they have got them, their anxiety is lest they should lose them.

3. "When they are anxious lest such things should be lost, there is nothing to which they will not proceed."

CHAPTER XVI. 1. The Master said, "Anciently, men had three failings, which now perhaps are not to be found.

2. "The high-mindedness of antiquity showed itself in a disregard of small things; the high-mindedness of the present day shows itself in wild license. The stern dignity of antiquity showed itself in grave reserve; the stern dignity of the present day shows itself in quarrelsome perverseness. The stupidity of antiquity showed itself in straightforwardness; the stupidity of the present day shows itself in sheer deceit."

CHAPTER XVII. The Master said, "Fine words and an insinuating appearance are seldom associated with virtue."

CHAPTER XVIII. The Master said, "I hate the manner in which purple takes away the luster of vermilion. I hate the way in which the songs of Chang confound the music of the Ya. I hate those who with their sharp mouths overthrow kingdoms and families."

CHAPTER XIX. 1. The Master said, "I would prefer not speaking."

2. Tsze-kung said, "If you, Master, do not speak, what shall we, your disciples, have to record?"

3. The Master said, "Does Heaven speak? The four seasons pursue their courses, and all things are continually being produced, but does Heaven say anything?"

CHAPTER XX. Zu Pei wished to see Confucius, but Confucius declined, on the ground of being sick, to see him. When the bearer of this message went out at the door, the Master took his lute and sang to it, in order that Pei might hear him.

CHAPTER XXI. 1. Tsai Wo asked about the three years' mourning for parents, saying that one year was long enough.

2. "If the superior man," said he, "abstains for three years from the observances of propriety, those observances will be quite lost. If for three years he abstains from music, music will be ruined.

3. "Within a year the old grain is exhausted, and the new grain has sprung up, and, in procuring fire by friction, we go through all the changes of wood for that purpose. After a complete year, the mourning may stop."

4. The Master said, "If you were, after a year, to eat good rice, and wear embroidered clothes, would you feel at ease?" "I should," replied Wo.

5. The Master said, "If you can feel at ease, do it. But a superior man, during the whole period of mourning, does not enjoy pleasant food which he may eat, nor derive pleasure from music which he may hear. He also does not feel at ease, if he is comfortably lodged. Therefore he does not do what you propose. But now you feel at ease and may do it."

6. Tsai Wo then went out, and the Master said, "This shows Yu's want of virtue. It is not till a child is three years old that it is allowed to leave the arms of its parents. And the three years' mourning is universally observed throughout the empire. Did Yu enjoy the three years' love of his parents?"

CHAPTER XXII. The Master said, "Hard is it to deal with him who will stuff himself with food the whole day, without applying his mind to anything good! Are there not gamesters and chess players? To be one of these would still be better than doing nothing at all."

CHAPTER XXIII. Tsze-lu said, "Does the superior man esteem valour?" The Master said, "The superior man holds righteousness to be of highest importance. A man in a superior situation, having valour without righteousness, will be guilty of insubordination; one of the lower people, having valour without righteousness, will commit robbery."

CHAPTER XXIV. 1. Tsze-kung said, "Has the superior man his hatreds also?" The Master said, "He has his hatreds. He hates those who proclaim the evil of others. He hates the man who, being in a low station, slanders his superiors. He hates those who have valour merely, and are unobservant of propriety. He hates those who are forward and determined, and, at the same time, of contracted understanding."

2. The Master then inquired, "Ts'ze, have you also your hatreds?" Tsze-kung replied, "I hate those who pry out matters, and ascribe the knowledge to their wisdom. I hate those who are only not modest, and think that they are valourous. I hate those who make known secrets, and think that they are straightforward."

CHAPTER XXV. The Master said, "Of all people, girls and servants are the most difficult to behave to. If you are familiar with them, they lose their humility. If you maintain a reserve towards them, they are discontented."

CHAPTER XXVI. The Master said, "When a man at forty is the object of dislike, he will always continue what he is."

Book XVIII

WEI TSZE

CHAPTER I. 1. The Viscount of Wei withdrew from the court. The Viscount of Chi became a slave to Chau. Pi-kan remonstrated with him and died.

2. Confucius said, "The Yin dynasty possessed these three men of virtue."

CHAPTER II. Hui of Liu-hsia, being chief criminal judge, was thrice dismissed from his office. Someone said to him, "Is it not yet time for you, sir, to leave this?" He replied, "Serving men in an upright way, where shall I go to and not experience such a thrice-repeated dismissal? If I choose to serve men in a crooked way, what necessity is there for me to leave the country of my parents?"

CHAPTER III. The Duke Ching of Ch'i, with reference to the manner in which he should treat Confucius, said, "I cannot treat him as I would the chief of the Chi family. I will treat him in a manner between that accorded to the chief of the Chi, and that given to the chief of the Mang family." He also said, "I am old; I cannot use his doctrines." Confucius took his departure.

CHAPTER IV. The people of Ch'i sent to Lu a present of female musicians, which Chi Hwan received, and for three days no court was held. Confucius took his departure.

CHAPTER V. 1. The madman of Ch'u, Chieh-yu, passed by Confucius, singing and saying, "O FANG! O FANG! How is your virtue degenerated! As to the past, reproof is useless; but the future may still be provided against. Give up your vain pursuit. Give up your vain pursuit. Peril awaits those who now engage in affairs of government."

2. Confucius alighted and wished to converse with him, but Chieh-yu hastened away, so that he could not talk with him.

CHAPTER VI. 1. Ch'ang-tsu and Chieh-ni were at work in the field together, when Confucius passed by them, and sent Tsze-lu to inquire for the ford.

2. Ch'ang-tsu said, "Who is he that holds the reins in the carriage there?" Tsze-lu told him, "It is K'ung Ch'iu." "Is it not K'ung Ch'iu of Lu?" asked he. "Yes," was the reply, to which the other rejoined, "He knows the ford."

3. Tsze-lu then inquired of Chieh-ni, who said to him, "Who are you, sir?" He answered, "I am Chung Yu." "Are you not the disciple of K'ung Ch'iu of Lu?" asked the other. "I am," replied he, and then Chieh-ni said to him, "Disorder, like a swelling flood, spreads over the whole empire, and who is he that will change its state for you? Than follow one who merely withdraws from this one

and that one, had you not better follow those who have withdrawn from the world altogether?" With this he fell to covering up the seed, and proceeded with his work, without stopping.

4. Tsze-lu went and reported their remarks, when the Master observed with a sigh, "It is impossible to associate with birds and beasts, as if they were the same with us. If I associate not with these people—with mankind—with whom shall I associate? If right principles prevailed through the empire, there would be no use for me to change its State."

CHAPTER VII. 1. Tsze-lu, following the Master, happened to fall behind, when he met an old man, carrying across his shoulder on a staff a basket for weeds. Tsze-lu said to him, "Have you seen my master, sir!" The old man replied, "Your four limbs are unaccustomed to toil; you cannot distinguish the five kinds of grain: who is your master?" With this, he planted his staff in the ground, and proceeded to weed.

2. Tsze-lu joined his hands across his breast, and stood before him.

3. The old man kept Tsze-lu to pass the night in his house, killed a fowl, prepared millet, and feasted him. He also introduced to him his two sons.

4. Next day, Tsze-lu went on his way, and reported his adventure. The Master said, "He is a recluse," and sent Tsze-lu back to see him again, but when he got to the place, the old man was gone.

5. Tsze-lu then said to the family, "Not to take office is not righteous. If the relations between old and young may not be neglected, how is it that he sets aside the duties that should be observed between sovereign and minister? Wishing to maintain

his personal purity, he allows that great relation to come to confusion. A superior man takes office, and performs the righteous duties belonging to it. As to the failure of right principles to make progress, he is aware of that."

CHAPTER VIII. 1. The men who have retired to privacy from the world have been Po-i, Shu-ch'i, Yu-chung, I-yi, Chu-chang, Hui of Liu-hsia, and Shao-lien.

2. The Master said, "Refusing to surrender their wills, or to submit to any taint in their persons—such, I think, were Po-i and Shu-ch'i.

3. "It may be said of Hui of Liu-hsia, and of Shao-lien, that they surrendered their wills, and submitted to taint in their persons, but their words corresponded with reason, and their actions were such as men are anxious to see. This is all that is to be remarked in them.

4. "It may be said of Yu-chung and I-yi that, while they hid themselves in their seclusion, they gave a license to their words; but, in their persons, they succeeded in preserving their purity, and, in their retirement, they acted according to the exigency of the times.

5. "I am different from all these. I have no course for which I am predetermined, and no course against which I am predetermined."

CHAPTER IX. 1. The grand music-master, Chih, went to Ch'i.

2. Kan, the master of the band at the second meal, went to Ch'u. Liao, the band master at the third meal, went to Ts'ai. Chueh, the band master at the fourth meal, went to Ch'in.

3. Fang-shu, the drum master, withdrew to the north of the river.

4. Wu, the master of the hand drum, withdrew to the Han.

5. Yang, the assistant music-master, and Hsiang, master of the musical stone, withdrew to an island in the sea.

CHAPTER X. The Duke of Chau addressed his son, the Duke of Lu, saying, "The virtuous prince does not neglect his relations. He does not cause the great ministers to repine at his not employing them. Without some great cause, he does not dismiss from their offices the members of old families. He does not seek in one man talents for every employment."

CHAPTER XI. To Chau belonged the eight officers, Po-ta, Po-kwo, Chung-tu, Chung-hwu, Shu-ya, Shu-hsia, Chi-sui, and Chi-kwa.

Book XIX

TSZE-CHANG

CHAPTER I. Tsze-chang said, "The scholar, trained for public duty, seeing threatening danger, is prepared to sacrifice his life. When the opportunity of gain is presented to him, he thinks of righteousness. In sacrificing, his thoughts are reverential. In mourning, his thoughts are about the grief which he should feel. Such a man commands our approbation indeed."

CHAPTER II. Tsze-chang said, "When a man holds fast to virtue, but without seeking to enlarge it, and believes right principles, but without firm sincerity, what account can be made of his existence or non-existence?"

CHAPTER III. The disciples of Tsze-hsia asked Tsze-chang about the principles that should characterize mutual intercourse. Tsze-chang asked, "What does Tsze-hsia say on the subject?" They replied, "Tsze-hsia says: 'Associate with those who can advantage you. Put away from you those who cannot do so.' " Tsze-chang observed, "This is different from what I have learned.

The superior man honours the talented and virtuous, and bears with all. He praises the good, and pities the incompetent. Am I possessed of great talents and virtue? Who is there among men whom I will not bear with? Am I devoid of talents and virtue? Men will put me away from them. What have we to do with the putting away of others?"

CHAPTER IV. Tsze-hsia said, "Even in inferior studies and employments there is something worth being looked at; but if it be attempted to carry them out to what is remote, there is a danger of their proving inapplicable. Therefore, the superior man does not practise them."

CHAPTER V. Tsze-hsia said, "He who from day to day recognises what he has not yet, and from month to month does not forget what he has attained to, may be said indeed to love to learn."

CHAPTER VI. Tsze-hsia said, "There are learning extensively, and having a firm and sincere aim; inquiring with earnestness, and reflecting with self-application: virtue is in such a course."

CHAPTER VII. Tsze-hsia said, "Mechanics have their shops to dwell in, in order to accomplish their works. The superior man learns, in order to reach to the utmost of his principles."

CHAPTER VIII. Tsze-hsia said, "The mean man is sure to gloss his faults."

CHAPTER IX. Tsze-hsia said, "The superior man undergoes three changes. Looked at from a distance, he appears stern; when approached, he is mild; when he is heard to speak, his language is firm and decided."

CHAPTER X. Tsze-hsia said, "The superior man, having obtained their confidence, may then impose labours on his people. If he have not gained their confidence, they will think that he is oppressing them. Having obtained the confidence of his prince, one may then remonstrate with him. If he have not gained his confidence, the prince will think that he is vilifying him."

CHAPTER XI. Tsze-hsia said, "When a person does not transgress the boundary line in the great virtues, he may pass and repass it in the small virtues."

CHAPTER XII. 1. Tsze-yu said, "The disciples and followers of Tsze-hsia, in sprinkling and sweeping the ground, in answering and replying, in advancing and receding, are sufficiently accomplished. But these are only the branches of learning, and they are left ignorant of what is essential. How can they be acknowledged as sufficiently taught?"

2. Tsze-hsia heard of the remark and said, "Alas! Yen Yu is wrong. According to the way of the superior man in teaching, what departments are there which he considers of prime importance, and delivers? What are there which he considers of secondary importance, and allows himself to be idle about? But as in the case of plants, which are assorted according to their classes, so he deals with his disciples. How can the way of a superior man be such as to make fools of any of them? Is it not the sage alone who can unite in one the beginning and the consummation of learning?"

CHAPTER XIII. Tsze-hsia said, "The officer, having discharged all his duties, should devote his leisure to learning. The student, having completed his learning, should apply himself to be an officer."

CHAPTER XIV. Tsze-hsia said, "Mourning, having been carried to the utmost degree of grief, should stop with that."

CHAPTER XV. Tsze-hsia said, "My friend Chang can do things which are hard to be done, but yet he is not perfectly virtuous."

CHAPTER XVI. The philosopher Tsang said, "How imposing is the manner of Chang! It is difficult along with him to practise virtue."

CHAPTER XVII. The philosopher Tsang said, "I heard this from our Master: 'Men may not have shown what is in them to the full extent, and yet they will be found to do so, on occasion of mourning for their parents.' "

CHAPTER XVIII. The philosopher Tsang said, "I have heard this from our Master: 'The filial piety of Mang Chwang, in other matters, was what other men are competent to, but, as seen in his not changing the ministers of his father, nor his father's mode of government, it is difficult to be attained to.' "

CHAPTER XIX. The chief of the Mang family having appointed Yang Fu to be chief criminal judge, the latter consulted the philosopher Tsang. Tsang said, "The rulers have failed in their duties, and the people consequently have been disorganised, for a long time. When you have found out the truth of any accusation, be grieved for and pity them, and do not feel joy at your own ability."

CHAPTER XX. Tsze-kung said, "Chau's wickedness was not so great as that name implies. Therefore, the superior man hates to dwell in a low-lying situation, where all the evil of the world will flow in upon him."

CHAPTER XXI. Tsze-kung said, "The faults of the superior man are like the eclipses of the sun and moon. He has his faults, and all men see them; he changes again, and all men look up to him."

CHAPTER XXII. 1. Kung-sun Ch'ao of Wei asked Tsze-kung, saying, "From whom did Chung-ni get his learning?"

2. Tsze-kung replied, "The doctrines of Wan and Wu have not yet fallen to the ground. They are to be found among men. Men of talents and virtue remember the greater principles of them, and others, not possessing such talents and virtue, remember the smaller. Thus, all possess the doctrines of Wan and Wu. Where could our Master go that he should not have an opportunity of learning them? And yet what necessity was there for his having a regular master?"

CHAPTER XXIII. 1. Shu-sun Wu-shu observed to the great officers in the court, saying, "Tsze-kung is superior to Chung-ni."

2. Tsze-fu Ching-po reported the observation to Tsze-kung, who said, "Let me use the comparison of a house and its encompassing wall. My wall only reaches to the shoulders. One may peep over it, and see whatever is valuable in the apartments.

3. "The wall of my Master is several fathoms high. If one do not find the door and enter by it, he cannot see the ancestral temple with its beauties, nor all the officers in their rich array.

4. "But I may assume that they are few who find the door. Was not the observation of the chief only what might have been expected?"

CHAPTER XXIV. Shu-sun Wu-shu having spoken revilingly of Chung-ni, Tsze-kung said, "It is of no use doing so. Chung-ni cannot be reviled. The talents and virtue of other men are hillocks and mounds which may be stepped over. Chung-ni is the sun or moon, which it is not possible to step over. Although a man may wish to cut himself off from the sage, what harm can he do to the sun or moon? He only shows that he does not know his own capacity."

CHAPTER XXV. 1. Ch'an Tsze-ch'in, addressing Tsze-kung, said, "You are too modest. How can Chung-ni be said to be superior to you?"

2. Tsze-kung said to him, "For one word a man is often deemed to be wise, and for one word he is often deemed to be foolish. We ought to be careful indeed in what we say.

3. "Our Master cannot be attained to, just in the same way as the heavens cannot be gone up to by the steps of a stair.

4. "Were our Master in the position of the ruler of a State or the chief of a family, we should find verified the description which has been given of a sage's rule: he would plant the people, and forthwith they would be established; he would lead them on, and forthwith they would follow him; he would make them happy, and forthwith multitudes would resort to his dominions; he would stimulate them, and forthwith they would be harmonious. While he lived, he would be glorious. When he died, he would be bitterly lamented. How is it possible for him to be attained to?"

Book XX

YAO YUEH

CHAPTER I. 1. Yao said, "Oh! You, Shun, the Heaven-determined order of succession now rests in your person. Sincerely hold fast the due Mean. If there shall be distress and want within the four seas, the Heavenly revenue will come to a perpetual end."

2. Shun also used the same language in giving charge to Yu.

3. T'ang said, "I, the child Li, presume to use a dark-coloured victim, and presume to announce to Thee, O most great and sovereign God, that the sinner I dare not pardon, and thy ministers, O God, I do not keep in obscurity. The examination of them is by thy mind, O God. If, in my person, I commit offences, they are not to be attributed to you, the people of the myriad regions. If you in the myriad regions commit offences, these offences must rest on my person."

4. Chau conferred great gifts, and the good were enriched.

5. "Although he has his near relatives, they are not equal to my virtuous men. The people are throwing blame upon me, the One man."

6. He carefully attended to the weights and measures, examined the body of the laws, restored the discarded officers, and the good government of the kingdom took its course.

7. He revived States that had been extinguished, restored families whose line of succession had been broken, and called to office those who had retired into obscurity, so that throughout the kingdom the hearts of the people turned towards him.

8. What he attached chief importance to were the food of the people, the duties of mourning, and sacrifices.

9. By his generosity, he won all. By his sincerity, he made the people repose trust in him. By his earnest activity, his achievements were great. By his justice, all were delighted.

CHAPTER II. 1. Tsze-chang asked Confucius, saying, "In what way should a person in authority act in order that he may conduct government properly?" The Master replied, "Let him honour the five excellent, and banish away the four bad, things; then may he conduct government properly." Tsze-chang said, "What are meant by the five excellent things?" The Master said, "When the person in authority is beneficent without great expenditure; when he lays tasks on the people without their repining; when he pursues what he desires without being covetous; when he maintains a dignified ease without being proud; when he is majestic without being fierce."

2. Tsze-chang said, "What is meant by being beneficent without great expenditure?" The Master replied, "When the person in

authority makes more beneficial to the people the things from which they naturally derive benefit—is not this being beneficent without great expenditure? When he chooses the labours which are proper, and makes them labour on them, who will repine? When his desires are set on benevolent government, and he secures it, who will accuse him of covetousness? Whether he has to do with many people or few, or with things great or small, he does not dare to indicate any disrespect; is not this to maintain a dignified ease without any pride? He adjusts his clothes and cap, and throws a dignity into his looks, so that, thus dignified, he is looked at with awe; is not this to be majestic without being fierce?"

3. Tsze-chang then asked, "What are meant by the four bad things?" The Master said, "To put the people to death without having instructed them—this is called cruelty. To require from them, suddenly, the full tale of work, without having given them warning—this is called oppression. To issue orders as if without urgency, at first, and, when the time comes, to insist on them with severity—this is called injury. And, generally, in the giving pay or rewards to men, to do it in a stingy way—this is called acting the part of a mere official."

CHAPTER III. 1. The Master said, "Without recognising the ordinances of Heaven, it is impossible to be a superior man.

2. "Without an acquaintance with the rules of Propriety, it is impossible for the character to be established.

3. "Without knowing the force of words, it is impossible to know men."

A Selection of the Sayings of Mencius

Book I

KING HWUY OF LEANG

PART I

Mencius went to see King Hwuy of Leang.[1] The king said, "Venerable Sir, since you have not counted it far to come here a distance of a thousand li, may I presume that you are likewise provided with counsels to profit my kingdom?" Mencius replied, "Why must your Majesty use that word 'profit'? What I am likewise provided with are counsels to benevolence and righteousness; and these are my only topics.

"If your Majesty say, 'What is to be done to profit my kingdom?' the great officers will say, 'What is to be done to profit our families?' and the inferior officers and the common people will say,

---

[1] The title of this book in Chinese is "King Hwuy of Leang; in chapters and sentences." Like the Books of the Confucian Analects, those of this work are headed by two or three words at or near the commencement of them. Each Book is divided into two parts. This arrangement was made by Chaou K'e, and to him are due also the divisions into chapters, and sentences, or paragraphs, containing, it may be, many sentences.

'What is to be done to profit our persons?' Superiors and inferiors will try to take the profit the one from the other, and the kingdom will be endangered. In the kingdom of ten thousand chariots, the murderer of his ruler will be the chief of a family of a thousand chariots. In the State of a thousand chariots, the murderer of his ruler will be the chief of a family of a hundred chariots. To have a thousand in ten thousand, and a hundred in a thousand, cannot be regarded as not a large allowance; but if righteousness be put last and profit first, they will not be satisfied without snatching all.

"There never was a man trained to benevolence who neglected his parents. There never was a man trained to righteousness who made his ruler an after consideration. Let your Majesty likewise make benevolence and righteousness your only themes—why must you speak of profit?"

When Mencius, another day, was seeing King Hwuy of Leang, the King went and stood with him by a pond, and, looking round on the wild geese and deer, large and small, said, "Do wise and good princes also take pleasure in these things?" Mencius replied, "Being wise and good, they then have pleasure in these things. If they are not wise and good, though they have these things, they do not find pleasure. It is said in the 'Book of Poetry':–

> When he planned the commencement of the Marvellous
> Tower,
> He planned it, and defined it,
> And the people in crowds undertook the work,
> And in no time completed it.
> When he planned the commencement, he said, "Be not
> in a hurry."
> But the people came as if they were his children.
> The king was in the Marvellous Park,

Where the does were lying down—
The does so sleek and fat;
With the white birds glistening.
The king was by the Marvellous Pond;–
How full was it of fishes leaping about!

King Wan used the strength of the people to make his tower and pond, and the people rejoiced to do the work, calling the tower 'the Marvellous Tower,' and the pond 'the Marvellous Pond,' and being glad that he had his deer, his fishes and turtles. The ancients caused their people to have pleasure as well as themselves, and therefore they could enjoy it.

"In the Declaration of T'ang it is said, 'O Sun, when wilt thou expire? We will die together with thee.' The people wished for Keeh's death, though they should die with him. Although he had his tower, his pond, birds and animals, how could he have pleasure alone?"

King Hwuy of Leang said, "Small as my virtue is, in the government of my kingdom, I do indeed exert my mind to the utmost. If the year be bad inside the Ho, I remove as many of the people as I can to the east of it, and convey grain to the country inside. If the year be bad on the east of the river, I act on the same plan. On examining the governmental methods of the neighboring kingdoms, I do not find there is any ruler who exerts his mind as I do. And yet the people of the neighboring kings do not decrease, nor do my people increase—how is this?"

Mencius replied, "Your Majesty loves war; allow me to take an illustration from war. The soldiers move forward at the sound of the drum; and when the edges of their weapons have been crossed, on one side, they throw away their buff coats, trail their weapons behind them, and run. Some run a hundred paces and then stop; some run fifty paces and stop. What would you think if these, because they had run but fifty paces, should laugh at those who ran a hundred paces?" The king said, "They cannot do so. They only did not run a hundred paces; but they also ran." Mencius said, "Since your Majesty knows this you have no ground to expect that your people will become more numerous than those of the neighboring kingdoms.

"If the seasons of husbandry be not interfered with, the grain will be more than can be eaten. If close nets are not allowed to enter the pools and ponds, the fish and turtles will be more than can be consumed. If the axes and bills enter the hill-forests only at the proper times, the wood will be more than can be used. When the grain and fish and turtles are more than can be eaten, and there is more wood than can be used, this enables the people to nourish their living and do all offices for their dead, without any feeling against any. But this condition, in which the people nourish their living, and do all offices to their dead without having any feeling against any, is the first step in the Royal way.

"Let mulberry trees be planted about the homesteads with their five acres, and persons of fifty years will be able to wear silk. In keeping fowls, pigs, dogs, and swine, let not their time of breeding be neglected, and persons of seventy years will be able to eat flesh. Let there not be taken away the time that is proper for the cultivation of the field allotment of a hundred acres, and the family of several mouths will not suffer from hunger. Let careful attention be paid to the teaching in the various schools, with repeated inculcation of the filial and fraternal duties, and gray-haired men will not be seen upon the roads, carrying burdens on their backs or on their heads. It has never been that the ruler of a State where these results were seen, persons of seventy wearing silk and eating flesh, and the black-haired people suffering neither from hunger nor cold, did not attain to the Royal dignity.

"Your dogs and swine eat the food of men, and you do not know to store up of the abundance. There are people dying from famine on the roads, and you do not know to issue your stores for their relief. When men die, you say, 'It is not owing to me; it is owing to the year.' In what does this differ from stabbing a man and killing him, and then saying, 'It was not I; it was the weapon'? Let your Majesty cease to lay the blame on the year and instantly the people, all under the sky, will come to you."

King Hwuy of Leang said, "I wish quietly to receive your instructions." Mencius replied, "Is there any difference between killing a man with a stick and with a sword?" "There is no difference," was the answer.

Mencius continued, "Is there any difference between doing it with a sword and with governmental measures?" "There is not," was the answer again.

Mencius then said, "In your stalls there are fat beasts; in your stables there are fat horses. But your people have the look of hunger, and in the fields there are those who have died of famine. This is leading on beasts to devour men. Beasts devour one another, and men hate them for doing so. When he who is called the parent of the people conducts his government so as to be chargeable with leading on beasts to devour men, where is that parental relation to the people? Chung-ne said, 'Was he not without posterity who first made wooden images to bury with the dead?' So he said, because that man made the semblances of men and used them for that purpose; what shall be thought of him who causes his people to die of hunger?"

King Hwuy of Leang said, "There was not in the kingdom a stronger State than Ts'in, as you, venerable Sir, know. But since it descended to me, on the east we were defeated by Ts'e, and then my eldest son perished; on the west we lost seven hundred li of territory to Ts'in; and on the south we have sustained disgrace at the hands of Ts'oo. I have brought shame on my departed predecessors, and wish on their account to wipe it away once for all. What course is to be pursued to accomplish this?"

Mencius replied, "With a territory only a hundred li square it has been possible to obtain the Royal dignity. If your Majesty will indeed dispense a benevolent government to the people, being sparing in the use of punishments and fines, and making the taxes and levies of produce light, so causing that the fields shall be ploughed deep, and the weeding well attended to, and that the able-bodied, during their days of leisure, shall cultivate their filial piety, fraternal duty, faithfulness, and truth, serving thereby, at home, their fathers and elder brothers, and, abroad, their elders and superiors, you will then have a people who can be employed with sticks which they have prepared to oppose the strong buff coats and sharp weapons of the troops of Ts'in and Ts'oo.

"The rulers of those States rob their people of their time, so that they cannot plough and weed their fields in order to support their parents. Parents suffer from cold and hunger; elder and younger brothers, wives and children, are separated and scattered abroad. Those rulers drive their people into pitfalls or into the water; and your Majesty will go to punish them. In such a case, who will oppose your Majesty? In accordance with this is the saying, 'The benevolent has no enemy!' I beg your Majesty not to doubt what I said."

Mencius had an interview with King Seang[2] of Leang. When he came out he said to some persons, "When I looked at him from a distance, he did not appear like a ruler; when I drew near to him, I saw nothing venerable about him. Abruptly he asked me, 'How can the kingdom, all under the sky, be settled?' I replied, 'It will be settled by being united under one sway.'"

" 'Who can so unite it?' he asked.

"I replied, 'He who has no pleasure in killing men can so unite it.'

" 'Who can give it to him?' he asked.

"I replied, 'All under heaven will give it to him. Does your Majesty know the way of the growing grain? During the seventh and eighth months, when drought prevails, the plants become dry. Then the clouds collect densely in the heavens, and send down torrents of rain, so that the grain erects itself as if by a shoot. When it does so, who can keep it back? Now among those who are shepherds of men throughout the kingdom, there is not one who does not find pleasure in killing men. If there were one who did not find pleasure in killing men, all the people under the sky would be looking towards him with outstretched necks. Such being indeed the case, the people would go to him as water flows downwards with a rush, which no one can repress.'

King Seuen of Ts'e asked, saying, "May I be informed by you of the transactions of Hwan of Ts'e and Wan of Ts'in?"

---

[2] Seang was the son of King Hwuy. The first year of his reign is supposed to be B.C. 317. Seang's name was Hih. As a posthumous epithet, Seang has various meanings: "Land-enlarger and Virtuous"; "Successful in Arms." The interview here recorded seems to have taken place immediately after Hih's accession, and Mencius, it is said, was so disappointed by it that he soon after left the country.

Mencius replied, "There were none of the disciples of Chung-ne who spoke about the affairs of Hwan and Wan, and therefore they have not been transmitted to these after-ages; your servant has not heard of them. If you will have me speak, let it be about the principles of attaining to the Royal sway."

The king said, "Of what kind must his virtue be who can attain to the Royal sway?" Mencius said, "If he loves and protects the people, it is impossible to prevent him from attaining it."

The king said, "Is such an one as poor I competent to love and protect the people?" "Yes," was the reply. "From what do you know that I am competent to that?" "I have heard," said Mencius, "from Hoo Heih the following incident: 'The king,' said he, 'was sitting aloft in the hall, when some people appeared leading a bull past below it. The king saw it, and asked where the bull was going, and being answered that they were going to consecrate a bell with its blood, he said, "Let it go, I cannot bear its frightened appearance— as if it were an innocent person going to the place of death." They asked in reply whether, if they did so, they should omit the consecration of the bell, but the king said, "How can that be omitted? Change it for a sheep." ' I do not know whether this incident occurred."

"It did," said the king, and Mencius replied, "The heart seen in this is sufficient to carry you to the Royal sway. The people all supposed that your Majesty grudged the animal, but your servant knows surely that it was your Majesty's not being able to bear the sight of the creature's distress which made you do as you did."

The king said, "You are right; and yet there really was an appearance of what the people imagined. But though Ts'e be narrow and small, how should I grudge a bull? Indeed it was because I could not bear its frightened appearance, as if it were an innocent person going to the place of death, that therefore I changed it for a sheep."

Mencius said, "Let not your Majesty deem it strange that the people should think you grudged the animal. When you changed a large one for a small, how should they know the true reason? If you felt pained by its being led without any guilt to the place of death, what was there to choose between a bull and a sheep?" The king laughed and said, "What really was my mind in the matter? I did not grudge the value of the bull, and yet I changed it for a sheep! There was reason in the people's saying that I grudged the creature."

Mencius said, "There is no harm in their saying so. It was an artifice of benevolence. You saw the bull, and had not seen the sheep. So is the superior man affected towards animals, that, having seen them alive, he cannot bear to see them die, and, having heard their dying cries, he cannot bear to eat their flesh. On this account he keeps away from his stalls and kitchen."

The king was pleased and said, "The Ode says,

What other men have in their minds,
I can measure by reflection.

This might be spoken of you, my Master. I indeed did the thing, but when I turned my thoughts inward and sought for it, I could not discover my own mind. When you, Master, spoke those words, the movements of compassion began to work in my mind. But how is it that this heart has in it what is equal to the attainment of the Royal sway?"

149

Mencius said, "Suppose a man were to make this statement to your Majesty, 'My strength is sufficient to lift three thousand catties, but is not sufficient to lift one feather; my eyesight is sharp enough to examine the point of an autumn hair, but I do not see a wagon-load of fagots,' would your Majesty allow what he said?" "No," was the king's remark, and Mencius proceeded, "Now here is kindness sufficient to reach to animals, and yet no benefits are extended from it to the people—how is this? is an exception to be made here? The truth is, the feather's not being lifted is because the strength was not used; the wagon-load of firewood's not being seen is because the eyesight was not used; and the people's not being loved and protected is because the kindness is not used. Therefore your Majesty's not attaining to the Royal sway is because you do not do it, and not because you are not able to do it."

The king asked, "How may the difference between him who does not do a thing and him who is not able to do it be graphically set forth?" Mencius replied, "In such a thing as taking the T'ae mountain under your arm, and leaping with it over the North Sea, if you say to people, 'I am not able to do it,' that is a real case of not being able. In such a matter as breaking off a branch from a tree at the order of a superior, if you say to people, 'I am not able to do it,' it is not a case of not being able to do it. And so your Majesty's not attaining to the Royal sway is not such a case as that of taking the T'ae mountain under your arm and leaping over the North Sea with it; but it is a case like that of breaking off a branch from a tree.

"Treat with reverence due to age the elders in your own family, so that those in the families of others shall be similarly treated; treat with the kindness due to youth the young in your own family, so that those in the families of others shall be similarly treated—do this and the kingdom may be made to go round in your palm. It is said in the 'Book of Poetry,'

> His example acted on his wife,
> Extended to his brethren,
> And was felt by all the clans and States;

Telling us how King Wan simply took this kindly heart, and exercised it towards those parties. Therefore the carrying out of the feeling of kindness by a ruler will suffice for the love and protection of all within the four seas; and if he do not carry it out, he will not be able to protect his wife and children. The way in which the ancients came greatly to surpass other men was no other than this, that they carried out well what they did, so as to affect others. Now your kindness is sufficient to reach to animals, and yet no benefits are extended from it to the people. How is this? Is an exception to be made here?

"By weighing we know what things are light, and what heavy. By measuring we know what things are long, and what short. All things are so dealt with, and the mind requires specially to be so. I beg your Majesty to measure it.Your Majesty collects your equipments of war, endangers your soldiers and officers and excites the resentment of the various princes—do these things cause you pleasure in your mind?"

The king said, "No. How should I derive pleasure from these things? My object in them is to seek for what I greatly desire."

Mencius said, "May I hear from you what it is that your Majesty greatly desires?" The king laughed, and did not speak. Mencius resumed, "Are you led to desire it because you have not enough of rich and sweet food for your mouth? Or because you have not enough of light and warm clothing for your body? Or because you have not enough of beautifully coloured objects to satisfy your eyes? Or because there are not voices and sounds enough to fill your ears? Or because you have not enough of attendants and favorites to stand before you and receive your orders? Your Majesty's various officers are sufficient to supply you with all these things. How can your Majesty have such a desire on account of them?" "No," said the king, "my desire is not on account of them." Mencius observed, "Then what your Majesty greatly desires can be known. You desire to enlarge your territories, to have Ts'in and Ts'oo coming to your court, to rule the Middle States, and to attract to you the barbarous tribes that surround them. But to do what you do in order to seek for what you desire is like climbing a tree to seek for fish."

"Is it so bad as that?" said the king. "I apprehend it is worse," was the reply. "If you climb a tree to seek for fish, although you do not get the fish, you have no subsequent calamity. But if you do what you do in order to seek for what you desire, doing it even with all your heart, you will assuredly afterwards meet with calamities." The king said, "May I hear what they will be?" Mencius replied, "If the people of Tsow were fighting with the people of Ts'oo, which of them does your Majesty think would conquer?" "The people of Ts'oo would conquer," was the answer, and Mencius pursued, "So then, a small State cannot contend with a great, few cannot contend with many, nor can the weak contend with the strong. The territory within the seas would embrace nine divisions, each of a thousand li square. All Ts'e together is one of them. If with one part you try to subdue the other eight, what is the difference between that and Tsow's contending with Ts'oo? With the desire which you have, you must turn back to the proper course for its attainment.

"Now, if your Majesty will institute a government whose action shall all be benevolent, this will cause all the officers in the kingdom to wish to stand in your Majesty's court, the farmers all to wish to plough in your Majesty's fields, the merchants, both travelling and stationary, all to wish to store their goods in your Majesty's market-places, travellers and visitors all to wish to travel on your Majesty's roads, and all under heaven who feel aggrieved by their rulers to wish to come and complain to your Majesty. When they are so bent, who will be able to keep them back?"

The king said, "I am stupid and cannot advance to this. But I wish you, my Master, to assist my intentions. Teach me clearly, and although I am deficient in intelligence and vigour, I should like to try at least to institute such a government."

Mencius replied, "They are only men of education who, without a certain livelihood, are able to maintain a fixed heart. As to the people, if they have not a certain livelihood, they will be found not to have a fixed heart. And if they have not a fixed heart, there is nothing which they will not do in the way of self-abandonment, of moral deflection, of depravity, and of wild license. When they have thus been involved in crime, to follow them up and punish them is to entrap the people. How can such a thing as entrapping the people be done under the rule of a benevolent man?

"Therefore, an intelligent ruler will regulate the livelihood of the people, so as to make sure that, above, they shall have sufficient wherewith to serve their parents, and below, sufficient wherewith to support their wives and children; that in good years they shall always be abundantly satisfied, and that in bad years they shall not be in danger of perishing. After this he may urge them, and they will proceed to what is good, for in this case the people will follow after that with readiness.

"But now the livelihood of the people is so regulated that, above, they have not sufficient wherewith to serve their parents, and, below, they have not sufficient wherewith to support their wives and children; even in good years their lives are always embittered, and in bad years they are in danger of perishing. In such circumstances their only object is to escape from death, and they are afraid they will not succeed in doing so—what leisure have they to cultivate propriety and righteousness?

"If your Majesty wishes to carry out a benevolent government, why not turn back to what is the essential step to its attainment?

"Let mulberry trees be planted about the homesteads with their five acres, and persons of fifty years will be able to wear silk. In keeping fowls, pigs, dogs, and swine, let not their times of breeding be neglected, and persons of seventy years will be able to eat flesh. Let there not be taken away the time that is proper for the cultivation of the field-allotment of a hundred acres, and the family of eight mouths will not suffer from hunger. Let careful attention be paid to the teaching in the various schools, with repeated inculcation of the filial and fraternal duties, and gray-haired men will not be seen upon the roads, carrying burdens on their backs or on their heads. It has never been that the ruler of a State, where these results were seen, the old wearing silk and eating flesh, and the black-haired people suffering neither from hunger nor cold, did not attain to the Royal dignity."

The Way and Its
Power of Laozi

PART I

CHAPTER I. 1. The Tao that can be trodden is not the enduring and unchanging Tao. The name that can be named is not the enduring and unchanging name.

2. Conceived of as having no name, it is the Originator of Heaven and Earth; conceived of as having a name, it is the Mother of all things.

3. Always without desire we must be found,
   If its deep mystery we would sound;
   But if desire always within us be,
   Its outer fringe is all that we shall see.

4. Under these two aspects, it is really the same; but as development takes place, it receives the different names. Together we call them the Mystery. Where the Mystery is the deepest is the gate of all that is subtle and wonderful.

CHAPTER 2. 1. All in the world know the beauty of the beautiful, and in doing this they have the idea of what ugliness is; they all know the skill of the skilful, and in doing this they have the idea of what the want of skill is.

2. So it is that existence and non-existence give birth the one to the idea of the other; that difficulty and ease produce the one the idea of the other; that length and shortness fashion out the one the figure of the other; that the ideas of height and lowness arise from the contrast of the one with the other; that the musical notes and tones become harmonious through the relation of one with another; and that being before and behind give the idea of one following another.

3. Therefore the sage manages affairs without doing anything, and conveys his instructions without the use of speech.

4. All things spring up, and there is not one which declines to show itself; they grow, and there is no claim made for their ownership; they go through their processes, and there is no expectation of a reward for the results. The work is accomplished, and there is no resting in it as an achievement.

The work is done, but how no one can see;
'Tis this that makes the power not cease to be.

CHAPTER 3. 1. Not to value and employ men of superior ability is the way to keep the people from rivalry among themselves; not to prize articles which are difficult to procure is the way to keep them from becoming thieves; not to show them what is likely to excite their desires is the way to keep their minds from disorder.

2. Therefore the sage, in the exercise of his government, empties their minds, fills their bellies, weakens their wills, and strengthens their bones.

3. He constantly tries to keep them without knowledge and without desire, and where there are those who have knowledge, to keep them from presuming to act on it. When there is this abstinence from action, good order is universal.

CHAPTER 4. 1. The Tao is like the emptiness of a vessel; and in our employment of it we must be on our guard against all fulness. How deep and unfathomable it is, as if it were the Honoured Ancestor of all things!

2. We should blunt our sharp points, and unravel the complications of things; we should attemper our brightness, and bring ourselves into agreement with the obscurity of others. How pure and still the Tao is, as if it would ever so continue!

3. I do not know whose son it is. It might appear to have been before God.

CHAPTER 5. 1. Heaven and Earth do not act from the impulse of any wish to be benevolent; they deal with all things as the dogs of grass are dealt with. The sages do not act from any wish to be benevolent; they deal with the people as the dogs of grass are dealt with.

2. May not the space between Heaven and Earth be compared to a bellows?
    'Tis emptied, yet it loses not its power;
    'Tis moved again, and sends forth air the more.
    Much speech to swift exhaustion lead we see;
    Your inner being guard, and keep it free.

6. The valley spirit dies not, aye the same;
    The female mystery thus do we name.

Its gate, from which at first they issued forth,
Is called the root from which grew Heaven and Earth.
Long and unbroken does its power remain,
Used gently, and without the touch of pain.

CHAPTER 7. 1. Heaven is long-enduring and Earth continues long. The reason why Heaven and Earth are able to endure and continue thus long is because they do not live of, or for, themselves. This is how they are able to continue and endure.

2. Therefore the sage puts his own person last, and yet it is found in the foremost place; he treats his person as if it were foreign to him, and yet that person is preserved. Is it not because he has no personal and private ends that therefore such ends are realised?

CHAPTER 8. 1. The highest excellence is like that of water. The excellence of water appears in its benefiting all things, and in its occupying, without striving to the contrary, the low place which all men dislike. Hence its way is near to that of the Tao.

2. The excellence of a residence is in the suitability of the place; that of the mind is in abysmal stillness; that of associations is in their being with the virtuous; that of government is in its securing good order; that of the conduct of affairs is in its ability; and that of the initiation of any movement is in its timeliness.

3. And when one with the highest excellence does not wrangle about his low position, no one finds fault with him.

CHAPTER 9. 1. It is better to leave a vessel unfilled than to attempt to carry it when it is full. If you keep feeling a point that has been sharpened, the point cannot long preserve its sharpness.

2. When gold and jade fill the hall, their possessor cannot keep them safe. When wealth and honours lead to arrogancy, this brings its evil on itself. When the work is done, and one's name is becoming distinguished, to withdraw into obscurity is the Way of Heaven.

CHAPTER 10. 1. When the intelligent and animal souls are held together in one embrace, they can be kept from separating. When one gives undivided attention to the vital breath, and brings it to the utmost degree of pliancy, he can become as a tender babe. When he has cleansed away the most mysterious sights of his imagination, he can become without a flaw.

2. In loving the people and ruling the state, cannot he proceed without any purpose of action? In the opening and shutting of his gates of Heaven, cannot he do so as a female bird? While his intelligence reaches in every direction, cannot he appear to be without knowledge?

3. The Tao produces all things and nourishes them; it produces them and does not claim them as its own; it does all, and yet does not boast of it; it presides over all, and yet does not control them. This is what is called "The mysterious Quality" of the Tao.

CHAPTER 11. The thirty spokes unite in the one nave; but it is on the empty space for the axle that the use of the wheel depends. Clay is fashioned into vessels; but it is on their empty hollowness that their use depends. The door and windows are cut out from the walls to form an apartment; but it is on the empty space within that its use depends. Therefore, what has a positive existence serves for profitable adaptation, and what has not that for actual usefulness.

CHAPTER 12. 1.
　　Colour's five hues from th' eyes their sight will take;
　　Music's five notes the ears as deaf can make;
　　The flavours five deprive the mouth of taste;
　　The chariot course, and the wild hunting waste
　　Make mad the mind; and objects rare and strange,
　　Sought for, men's conduct will to evil change.

2. Therefore the sage seeks to satisfy the craving of the belly, and not the insatiable longing of the eyes. He puts from him the latter, and prefers to seek the former.

CHAPTER 13. 1. Favour and disgrace would seem equally to be feared; honour and great calamity, to be regarded as personal conditions of the same kind.

2. What is meant by speaking thus of favour and disgrace? Disgrace is being in a low position after the enjoyment of favour. The getting that favour leads to the apprehension of losing it, and the losing it leads to the fear of still greater calamity—this is what is meant by saying that favour and disgrace would seem equally to be feared.

And what is meant by saying that honour and great calamity are to be similarly regarded as personal conditions? What makes me liable to great calamity is my having the body which I call myself; if I had not the body, what great calamity could come to me?

3. Therefore he who would administer the kingdom, honouring it as he honours his own person, may be employed to govern it, and he who would administer it with the love which he bears to his own person may be entrusted with it.

CHAPTER 14. 1. We look at it, and we do not see it, and we name it "the Equable." We listen to it, and we do not hear it,

161

and we name it "the Inaudible." We try to grasp it, and do not get hold of it, and we name it "the Subtle." With these three qualities, it cannot be made the subject of description; and hence we blend them together and obtain The One.

2. Its upper part is not bright, and its lower part is not obscure. Ceaseless in its action, it yet cannot be named, and then it again returns and becomes nothing. This is called the Form of the Formless, and the Semblance of the Invisible; this is called the Fleeting and Indeterminable.

3. We meet it and do not see its Front; we follow it, and do not see its Back. When we can lay hold of the Tao of old to direct the things of the present day, and are able to know it as it was of old in the beginning, this is called unwinding the clue of Tao.

CHAPTER 15. 1. The skilful masters of the Tao in old times, with a subtle and exquisite penetration, comprehended its mysteries, and were deep also so as to elude men's knowledge. As they were thus beyond men's knowledge, I will make an effort to describe of what sort they appeared to be.

2. Shrinking looked they like those who wade through a stream in winter; irresolute like those who are afraid of all around them; grave like a guest in awe of his host; evanescent like ice that is melting away; unpretentious like wood that has not been fashioned into anything; vacant like a valley, and dull like muddy water.

3. Who can make the muddy water clear? Let it be still, and it will gradually become clear. Who can secure the condition of rest? Let movement go on, and the condition of rest will gradually arise.

4. They who preserve this method of the Tao do not wish to be full of themselves. It is through their not being full of themselves

that they can afford to seem worn and not appear new and complete.

CHAPTER 16. 1. The state of vacancy should be brought to the utmost degree, and that of stillness guarded with unwearying vigour. All things alike go through their processes of activity, and then we see them return to their original state. When things in the vegetable world have displayed their luxuriant growth, we see each of them return to its root. This returning to their root is what we call the state of stillness; and that stillness may be called a reporting that they have fulfilled their appointed end.

2. The report of that fulfilment is the regular, unchanging rule. To know that unchanging rule is to be intelligent; not to know it leads to wild movements and evil issues. The knowledge of that unchanging rule produces a grand capacity and forbearance, and that capacity and forbearance lead to a community of feeling with all things. From this community of feeling comes a kingliness of character; and he who is king-like goes on to be Heaven-like. In that likeness to Heaven he possesses the Tao. Possessed of the Tao, he endures long; and to the end of his bodily life, is exempt from all danger of decay.

CHAPTER 17. 1. In the highest antiquity, the people did not know that there were their rulers. In the next age they loved them and praised them. In the next they feared them; in the next they despised them. Thus it was that when faith in the Tao was deficient in the rulers a want of faith in them ensued in the people.

2. How irresolute did those earliest rulers appear, showing by their reticence the importance which they set upon their words! Their work was done and their undertakings were successful, while the people all said, "We are as we are, of ourselves!"

CHAPTER 18. 1. When the Great Tao Way or Method ceased to be observed, benevolence and righteousness came into vogue. Then appeared wisdom and shrewdness, and there ensued great hypocrisy.

2. When harmony no longer prevailed throughout the six kinships, filial sons found their manifestation; when the states and clans fell into disorder, loyal ministers appeared.

CHAPTER 19. 1. If we could renounce our sageness and discard our wisdom, it would be better for the people a hundredfold. If we could renounce our benevolence and discard our righteousness, the people would again become filial and kindly. If we could renounce our artful contrivances and discard our scheming for gain, there would be no thieves nor robbers.

2. Those three methods of government
Thought olden ways in elegance did fail
And made these names their want of worth to veil;
But simple views, and courses plain and true
Would selfish ends and many lusts eschew.

CHAPTER 20. 1. When we renounce learning we have no troubles.

The ready "yes" and flattering "yea"—
Small is the difference they display.
But mark their issues, good and ill;
What space the gulf between shall fill?

What all men fear is indeed to be feared; but how wide and without end is the range of questions asking to be discussed!

2. The multitude of men look satisfied and pleased as if enjoying a full banquet, as if mounted on a tower in spring. I alone seem

listless and still, my desires having as yet given no indication of their presence. I am like an infant which has not yet smiled. I look dejected and forlorn, as if I had no home to go to. The multitude of men all have enough and to spare. I alone seem to have lost everything. My mind is that of a stupid man; I am in a state of chaos.

Ordinary men look bright and intelligent, while I alone seem to be benighted. They look full of discrimination, while I alone am dull and confused. I seem to be carried about as on the sea, drifting as if I had nowhere to rest. All men have their spheres of action, while I alone seem dull and incapable, like a rude borderer. Thus I alone am different from other men, but I value the nursing-mother the Tao.

CHAPTER 21.

    The grandest forms of active force
    From Tao come, their only source.
    Who can of Tao the nature tell?
    Our sight it flies, our touch as well.
    Eluding sight, eluding touch,
    The forms of things all in it crouch;
    Eluding touch, eluding sight,
    There are their semblances, all right.
    Profound it is, dark and obscure;
    Things' essences all there endure.
    Those essences the truth enfold
    Of what, when seen, shall then be told.
    Now it is so; 'twas so of old.
    Its name—what passes not away;
    So, in their beautiful array,
    Things form and never know decay.

How know I that it is so with all the beauties of existing things? By this nature of the Tao.

CHAPTER 22. 1. The partial becomes complete; the crooked, straight; the empty, full; the worn out, new. He whose desires are few gets them; he whose desires are many goes astray.

2. Therefore the sage holds in his embrace the one thing of humility, and manifests it to all the world. He is free from self-display, and therefore he shines; from self-assertion, and therefore he is distinguished; from self-boasting, and therefore his merit is acknowledged; from self-complacency, and therefore he acquires superiority. It is because he is thus free from striving that therefore no one in the world is able to strive with him.

3. That saying of the ancients that "the partial becomes complete" was not vainly spoken: all real completion is comprehended under it.

CHAPTER 23. 1. Abstaining from speech marks him who is obeying the spontaneity of his nature. A violent wind does not last for a whole morning; a sudden rain does not last for the whole day. To whom is it that these two things are owing? To Heaven and Earth. If Heaven and Earth cannot make such spasmodic actings last long, how much less can man!

2. Therefore when one is making the Tao his business, those who are also pursuing it agree with him in it, and those who are making the manifestation of its course their object agree with him in that; while even those who are failing in both these things agree with him where they fail.

3. Hence, those with whom he agrees as to the Tao have the happiness of attaining to it; those with whom he agrees as to its manifestation have the happiness of attaining to it; and those with whom he agrees in their failure have also the happiness of attaining

to the Tao. But when there is not faith sufficient on his part, a want of faith in him ensues on the part of the others.

CHAPTER 24. He who stands on his tiptoes does not stand firm; he who stretches his legs does not walk easily. So, he who displays himself does not shine; he who asserts his own views is not distinguished; he who vaunts himself does not find his merit acknowledged; he who is self-conceited has no superiority allowed to him. Such conditions, viewed from the standpoint of the Tao, are like remnants of food, or a tumour on the body, which all dislike. Hence those who pursue the course of the Tao do not adopt and allow them.

CHAPTER 25. 1. There was something undefined and complete, coming into existence before Heaven and Earth. How still it was and formless, standing alone, and undergoing no change, reaching everywhere and in no danger of being exhausted! It may be regarded as the Mother of all things.

2. I do not know its name, and I give it the designation of the Tao the Way or Course. Making an effort further to give it a name I call it The Great.

3. Great, it passes on in constant flow. Passing on, it becomes remote. Having become remote, it returns. Therefore the Tao is great; Heaven is great; Earth is great; and the sage king is also great. In the universe there are four that are great, and the sage king is one of them.

4. Man takes his law from the Earth; the Earth takes its law from Heaven; Heaven takes its law from the Tao. The law of the Tao is its being what it is.

CHAPTER 26. 1. Gravity is the root of lightness; stillness, the ruler of movement.

2. Therefore a wise prince, marching the whole day, does not go far from his baggage wagons. Although he may have brilliant prospects to look at, he quietly remains in his proper place, indifferent to them. How should the lord of a myriad chariots carry himself lightly before the kingdom? If he do act lightly, he has lost his root of gravity; if he proceed to active movement, he will lose his throne.

CHAPTER 27. 1. The skilful traveller leaves no traces of his wheels or footsteps; the skilful speaker says nothing that can be found fault with or blamed; the skilful reckoner uses no tallies; the skilful closer needs no bolts or bars, while to open what he has shut will be impossible; the skilful binder uses no strings or knots, while to unloose what he has bound will be impossible. In the same way the sage is always skilful at saving men, and so he does not cast away any man; he is always skilful at saving things, and so he does not cast away anything. This is called "Hiding the light of his procedure."

2. Therefore the man of skill is a master to be looked up to by him who has not the skill; and he who has not the skill is the helper of the reputation of him who has the skill. If the one did not honour his master, and the other did not rejoice in his helper, an observer, though intelligent, might greatly err about them. This is called "The utmost degree of mystery."

CHAPTER 28. 1.
Who knows his manhood's strength,
Yet still his female feebleness maintains;
As to one channel flow the many drains,

All come to him, yea, all beneath the sky.
Thus he the constant excellence retains;
The simple child again, free from all stains.

Who knows how white attracts,
Yet always keeps himself within black's shade,
The pattern of humility displayed,
Displayed in view of all beneath the sky;
He in the unchanging excellence arrayed,
Endless return to man's first state has made.

Who knows how glory shines,
Yet loves disgrace, nor e'er for it is pale;
Behold his presence in a spacious vale,
To which men come from all beneath the sky.
The unchanging excellence completes its tale;
The simple infant man in him we hail.

2. The unwrought material, when divided and distributed, forms vessels. The sage, when employed, becomes the Head of all the Officers of government; and in his greatest regulations he employs no violent measures.

CHAPTER 29. 1. If anyone should wish to get the kingdom for himself, and to effect this by what he does, I see that he will not succeed. The kingdom is a spirit-like thing, and cannot be got by active doing. He who w\ould so win it destroys it; he who would hold it in his grasp loses it.

2. The course and nature of things is such that
What was in front is now behind;
What warmed anon we freezing find.
Strength is of weakness oft the spoil;
The store in ruins mocks our toil.

Hence the sage puts away excessive effort, extravagance, and easy indulgence.

CHAPTER 30. 1. He who would assist a lord of men in harmony with the Tao will not assert his mastery in the kingdom by force of arms. Such a course is sure to meet with its proper return.

2. Wherever a host is stationed, briars and thorns spring up. In the sequence of great armies there are sure to be bad years.

3. A skilful commander strikes a decisive blow, and stops. He does not dare by continuing his operations to assert and complete his mastery. He will strike the blow, but will be on his guard against being vain or boastful or arrogant in consequence of it. He strikes it as a matter of necessity; he strikes it, but not from a wish for mastery.

4. When things have attained their strong maturity they become old. This may be said to be not in accordance with the Tao: and what is not in accordance with it soon comes to an end.

CHAPTER 31. 1. Now arms, however beautiful, are instruments of evil omen, hateful, it may be said, to all creatures. Therefore they who have the Tao do not like to employ them.

2. The superior man ordinarily considers the left hand the most honourable place, but in time of war the right hand. Those sharp weapons are instruments of evil omen, and not the instruments of the superior man—he uses them only on the compulsion of necessity. Calm and repose are what he prizes; victory by force of arms is to him undesirable. To consider this desirable would be to delight in the slaughter of men; and he who delights in the slaughter of men cannot get his will in the kingdom.

3. On occasions of festivity to be on the left hand is the prized position; on occasions of mourning, the right hand. The second in command of the army has his place on the left; the general commanding in chief has his on the right; his place, that is, is assigned to him as in the rites of mourning. He who has killed multitudes of men should weep for them with the bitterest grief; and the victor in battle has his place rightly according to those rites.

CHAPTER 32. 1. The Tao, considered as unchanging, has no name.

2. Though in its primordial simplicity it may be small, the whole world dares not deal with one embodying it as a minister. If a feudal prince or the king could guard and hold it, all would spontaneously submit themselves to him.

3. Heaven and Earth under its guidance unite together and send down the sweet dew, which, without the directions of men, reaches equally everywhere as of its own accord.

4. As soon as it proceeds to action, it has a name. When it once has that name, men can know to rest in it. When they know to rest in it, they can be free from all risk of failure and error.

5. The relation of the Tao to all the world is like that of the great rivers and seas to the streams from the valleys.

CHAPTER 33. 1. He who knows other men is discerning; he who knows himself is intelligent. He who overcomes others is strong; he who overcomes himself is mighty. He who is satisfied with his lot is rich; he who goes on acting with energy has a firm will.

2. He who does not fail in the requirements of his position continues long; he who dies and yet does not perish has longevity.

CHAPTER 34. 1. All-pervading is the Great Tao! It may be found on the left hand and on the right.

2. All things depend on it for their production, which it gives to them, not one refusing obedience to it. When its work is accomplished, it does not claim the name of having done it. It clothes all things as with a garment, and makes no assumption of being their lord—it may be named in the smallest things. All things return to their root and disappear, and do not know that it is it which presides over their doing so—it may be named in the greatest things.

3. Hence the sage is able in the same way to accomplish his great achievements. It is through his not making himself great that he can accomplish them.

CHAPTER 35. 1. To him who holds in his hands the Great Image of the invisible Tao, the whole world repairs. Men resort to him, and receive no hurt, but find rest, peace, and the feeling of ease.

2. Music and dainties will make the passing guest stop for a time. But though the Tao as it comes from the mouth seems insipid and has no flavour, though it seems not worth being looked at or listened to, the use of it is inexhaustible.

CHAPTER 36. 1. When one is about to take an inspiration, he is sure to make a previous expiration; when he is going to weaken another, he will first strengthen him; when he is going to overthrow another, he will first have raised him up; when he is going to despoil another, he will first have made gifts to him: this is called "Hiding the light of his procedure."

2. The soft overcomes the hard; and the weak the strong.

3. Fishes should not be taken from the deep; instruments for the profit of a state should not be shown to the people.

CHAPTER 37. 1. The Tao in its regular course does nothing for the sake of doing it, and so there is nothing which it does not do.

2. If princes and kings were able to maintain it, all things would of themselves be transformed by them.

3. If this transformation became to me an object of desire, I would express the desire by the nameless simplicity.

Simplicity without a name
Is free from all external aim.
With no desire, at rest and still,
All things go right as of their will.

PART II

CHAPTER 38. 1. Those who possessed in highest degree the attributes of the Tao did not seek to show them, and therefore they possessed them in fullest measure. Those who possessed in a lower degree those attributes sought how not to lose them, and therefore they did not possess them in fullest measure.

2. Those who possessed in the highest degree those attributes did nothing with a purpose, and had no need to do anything. Those who possessed them in a lower degree were always doing, and had need to be so doing.

3. Those who possessed the highest benevolence were always seeking to carry it out, and had no need to be doing so. Those who possessed the highest righteousness were always seeking to carry it out, and had need to be so doing.

4. Those who possessed the highest sense of propriety were always seeking to show it, and when men did not respond to it, they bared the arm and marched up to them.

5. Thus it was that when the Tao was lost, its attributes appeared; when its attributes were lost, benevolence appeared; when benevolence was lost, righteousness appeared; and when righteousness was lost, the proprieties appeared.

6. Now propriety is the attenuated form of leal-heartedness and good faith, and is also the commencement of disorder; swift apprehension is only a flower of the Tao, and is the beginning of stupidity.

7. Thus it is that the Great man abides by what is solid, and eschews what is flimsy; dwells with the fruit and not with the flower. It is thus that he puts away the one and makes choice of the other.

CHAPTER 39. 1. The things which from of old have got the One the Tao are

> Heaven which by it is bright and pure;
> Earth rendered thereby firm and sure;
> Spirits with powers by it supplied;
> Valleys kept full throughout their void
> All creatures which through it do live
> Princes and kings who from it get
> The model which to all they give.

All these are the results of the One Tao.

2. If Heaven were not thus pure, it soon would rend;
> If Earth were not thus sure, 'twould break and bend;
> Without these powers, the spirits soon would fail;
> If not so filled, the drought would parch each vale;
> Without that life, creatures would pass away;

Princes and kings, without that moral sway,
However grand and high, would all decay.

3. Thus it is that dignity finds its firm root in its previous
meanness, and what is lofty finds its stability in the lowness from
which it rises. Hence princes and kings call themselves
"Orphans," "Men of small virtue," and as "Carriages without a
nave." Is not this an acknowledgment that in their considering
themselves mean they see the foundation of their dignity? So it is
that in the enumeration of the different parts of a carriage we do
not come on what makes it answer the ends of a carriage. They
do not wish to show themselves elegant-looking as jade, but prefer
to be coarse-looking as an ordinary stone.

CHAPTER 40. 1. The movement of the Tao
    By contraries proceeds;
And weakness marks the course
    Of Tao's mighty deeds.

2. All things under Heaven sprang from It as existing and named;
that existence sprang from It as non-existent and not named.

Ch. 41. 1. Scholars of the highest class, when they hear about the
Tao, earnestly carry it into practice. Scholars of the middle class,
when they have heard about it, seem now to keep it and now to
lose it. Scholars of the lowest class, when they have heard about
it, laugh greatly at it. If it were not thus laughed at, it would not
be fit to be the Tao.

2. Therefore the sentence-makers have thus expressed themselves:

The Tao, when brightest seen, seems light to lack;
Who progress in it makes, seems drawing back;

Its even way is like a rugged track.
Its highest virtue from the vale doth rise;
Its greatest beauty seems to offend the eyes;
And he has most whose lot the least supplies.
Its firmest virtue seems but poor and low;
Its solid truth seems change to undergo;
Its largest square doth yet no corner show
A vessel great, it is the slowest made;
Loud is its sound, but never word it said;
A semblance great, the shadow of a shade.

3. The Tao is hidden, and has no name; but it is the Tao which is skilful at imparting to all things what they need and making them complete.

CHAPTER 42. 1. The Tao produced One; One produced Two; Two produced Three; Three produced All things. All things leave behind them the Obscurity out of which they have come, and go forward to embrace the Brightness into which they have emerged, while they are harmonised by the Breath of Vacancy.

2. What men dislike is to be orphans, to have little virtue, to be as carriages without naves; and yet these are the designations which kings and princes use for themselves. So it is that some things are increased by being diminished, and others diminished by being increased.

3. What other men thus teach, I also teach. The violent and strong do not die their natural death. I will make this the basis of my teaching.

CHAPTER 43. 1. The softest thing in the world dashes against and overcomes the hardest; that which has no substantial existence enters where there is no crevice. I know hereby what advantage belongs to doing nothing with a purpose.

2. There are few in the world who attain to the teaching without words, and the advantage arising from non-action.

CHAPTER 44. 1. Or fame or life,
　Which do you hold more dear?
 Or life or wealth,
　To which would you adhere?
 Keep life and lose those other things;
 Keep them and lose your life:–which brings
　Sorrow and pain more near?

2. Thus we may see,
　　Who cleaves to fame
　　Rejects what is more great;
　Who loves large stores
　　Gives up the richer state.

3. Who is content
　Needs fear no shame.
　Who knows to stop
　Incurs no blame.
　From danger free
　Long live shall he.

CHAPTER 45. 1.
　Who thinks his great achievements poor
　Shall find his vigour long endure.
　Of greatest fulness, deemed a void,
　Exhaustion ne'er shall stem the tide.
　Do thou what's straight still crooked deem;

Thy greatest art still stupid seem,
And eloquence a stammering scream.

2. Constant action overcomes cold; being still overcomes heat. Purity and stillness give the correct law to all under Heaven.

CHAPTER. 46. 1. When the Tao prevails in the world, they send back their swift horses to draw the dung-carts. When the Tao is disregarded in the world, the war-horses breed in the border lands.

2. There is no guilt greater than to sanction ambition; no calamity greater than to be discontented with one's lot; no fault greater than the wish to be getting. Therefore the sufficiency of contentment is an enduring and unchanging sufficiency.

CHAPTER 47. 1. Without going outside his door, one understands all that takes place under the sky; without looking out from his window, one sees the Tao of Heaven. The farther that one goes out from himself, the less he knows.

2. Therefore the sages got their knowledge without travelling; gave their right names to things without seeing them; and accomplished their ends without any purpose of doing so.

CHAPTER 48. 1. He who devotes himself to learning seeks from day to day to increase his knowledge; he who devotes himself to the Tao seeks from day to day to diminish his doing.

2. He diminishes it and again diminishes it, till he arrives at doing nothing on purpose. Having arrived at this point of non-action, there is nothing which he does not do.

3. He who gets as his own all under Heaven does so by giving himself no trouble with that end. If one take trouble with that end, he is not equal to getting as his own all under heaven.

CHAPTER 49. 1. The sage has no invariable mind of his own; he makes the mind of the people his mind.

2. To those who are good to me, I am good; and to those who are not good to me, I am also good—and thus all get to be good. To those who are sincere with me, I am sincere; and to those who are not sincere with me, I am also sincere—and thus all get to be sincere.

3. The sage has in the world an appearance of indecision, and keeps his mind in a state of indifference to all. The people all keep their eyes and ears directed to him, and he deals with them all as his children.

CHAPTER 50. 1. Men come forth and live; they enter again and die.

2. Of every ten three are ministers of life to themselves; and three are ministers of death.

3. There are also three in every ten whose aim is to live, but whose movements tend to the land or place of death. And for what reason? Because of their excessive endeavours to perpetuate life.

4. But I have heard that he who is skilful in managing the life entrusted to him for a time travels on the land without having to shun rhinoceros or tiger, and enters a host without having to avoid buff coat or sharp weapon. The rhinoceros finds no place in him into which to thrust its horn, nor the tiger a place in which

to fix its claws, nor the weapon a place to admit its point. And for what reason? Because there is in him no place of death.

CHAPTER 51. 1. All things are produced by the Tao, and nourished by its outflowing operation. They receive their forms according to the nature of each, and are completed according to the circumstances of their condition. Therefore all things without exception honour the Tao, and exalt its outflowing operation.

2. This honouring of the Tao and exalting of its operation is not the result of any ordination, but always a spontaneous tribute.

3. Thus it is that the Tao produces all things, nourishes them, brings them to their full growth, nurses them, completes them, matures them, maintains them, and overspreads them.

4. It produces them and makes no claim to the possession of them; it carries them through their processes and does not vaunt its ability in doing so; it brings them to maturity and exercises no control over them—this is called its mysterious operation.

CHAPTER 52. 1. The Tao which originated all under the sky is to be considered as the Mother of them all.

2. When the mother is found, we know what her children should be. When one knows that he is his mother's child, and proceeds to guard the qualities of the mother that belong to him, to the end of his life he will be free from all peril.

3. Let him keep his mouth closed, and shut up the portals of his nostrils, and all his life he will be exempt from laborious exertion. Let him keep his mouth open, and spend his breath in

the promotion of his affairs, and all his life there will be no safety for him.

4. The perception of what is small is the secret of clear-sightedness; the guarding of what is soft and tender is the secret of strength.

5. Who uses well his light,
   Reverting to its source so bright,
   Will from his body ward all blight,
   And hides the unchanging from men's sight.

CHAPTER 53. 1. If I were suddenly to become known, and put into a position to conduct a government according to the Great Tao, what I should be most afraid of would be a boastful display.

2. The Great Tao or Way is very level and easy; but people love the by-ways.

3. Their court-yards and buildings shall be well kept, but their fields shall be ill-cultivated, and their granaries very empty. They shall wear elegant and ornamented robes, carry a sharp sword at their girdle, pamper themselves in eating and drinking, and have a superabundance of property and wealth;–such princes may be called robbers and boasters. This is contrary to the Tao surely!

CHAPTER 54. 1.
   What Tao's skilful planter plants
   Can never be uptorn;
   What his skilful arms enfold,
   From him can ne'er be borne.

Sons shall bring in lengthening line,
Sacrifices to his shrine.

2. Tao when nursed within one's self,
    His vigour will make true;
And where the family it rules
    What riches will accrue!
The neighbourhood where it prevails
    In thriving will abound;
And when 'tis seen throughout the State,
    Good fortune will be found.
Employ it the kingdom o'er,
    And men thrive all around.

3. In this way the effect will be seen in the person, by the observation of different cases; in the family; in the neighbourhood; in the state; and in the kingdom.

4. How do I know that this effect is sure to hold thus all under the sky? By this method of observation.

CHAPTER 55. 1. He who has in himself abundantly the attributes of the Tao is like an infant. Poisonous insects will not sting him; fierce beasts will not seize him; birds of prey will not strike him.

2. The infant's bones are weak and its sinews soft, but yet its grasp is firm. It knows not yet the union of male and female, and yet its virile member may be excited—showing the perfection of its physical essence. All day long it will cry without its throat becoming hoarse—showing the harmony in its constitution.

3. To him by whom this harmony is known,
    The secret of the unchanging Tao is shown,
    And in the knowledge wisdom finds its throne.

All life-increasing arts to evil turn;
Where the mind makes the vital breath to burn,
False is the strength, and o'er it we should mourn.

4. When things have become strong, they then become old, which may be said to be contrary to the Tao. Whatever is contrary to the Tao soon ends.

CHAPTER 56. 1. He who knows the Tao does not care to speak about it; he who is ever ready to speak about it does not know it.

2. He who knows it will keep his mouth shut and close the portals of his nostrils. He will blunt his sharp points and unravel the complications of things; he will attemper his brightness, and bring himself into agreement with the obscurity of others. This is called "the Mysterious Agreement."

3. Such an one cannot be treated familiarly or distantly; he is beyond all consideration of profit or injury; of nobility or meanness: he is the noblest man under Heaven.

CHAPTER 57. 1. A state may be ruled by measures of correction; weapons of war may be used with crafty dexterity; but the kingdom is made one's own only by freedom from action and purpose.

2. How do I know that it is so? By these facts: In the kingdom the multiplication of prohibitive enactments increases the poverty of the people; the more implements to add to their profit that the people have, the greater disorder is there in the state and clan; the more acts of crafty dexterity that men possess, the more do strange contrivances appear; the more display there is of legislation, the more thieves and robbers there are.

3. Therefore a sage has said, "I will do nothing of purpose, and the people will be transformed of themselves; I will be fond of keeping still, and the people will of themselves become correct. I will take no trouble about it, and the people will of themselves become rich; I will manifest no ambition, and the people will of themselves attain to the primitive simplicity."

CHAPTER 58. 1.

The government that seems the most unwise,
Oft goodness to the people best supplies;
That which is meddling, touching everything,
Will work but ill, and disappointment bring.

Misery—happiness is to be found by its side! Happiness—misery lurks beneath it! Who knows what either will come to in the end?

2. Shall we then dispense with correction? The method of correction shall by a turn become distortion, and the good in it shall by a turn become evil. The delusion of the people on this point has indeed subsisted for a long time.

3. Therefore the sage is like a square which cuts no one with its angles; like a corner which injures no one with its sharpness. He is straightforward, but allows himself no license; he is bright, but does not dazzle.

CHAPTER 59. 1. For regulating the human in our constitution and rendering the proper service to the heavenly, there is nothing like moderation.

2. It is only by this moderation that there is effected an early return to man's normal state. That early return is what I call the repeated accumulation of the attributes of the Tao. With that

repeated accumulation of those attributes, there comes the subjugation of every obstacle to such return. Of this subjugation we know not what shall be the limit; and when one knows not what the limit shall be, he may be the ruler of a state.

3. He who possesses the mother of the state may continue long. His case is like that of the plant of which we say that its roots are deep and its flower stalks firm: this is the way to secure that its enduring life shall long be seen.

CHAPTER 60. 1. Governing a great state is like cooking small fish.

2. Let the kingdom be governed according to the Tao, and the manes of the departed will not manifest their spiritual energy. It is not that those manes have not that spiritual energy, but it will not be employed to hurt men. It is not that it could not hurt men, but neither does the ruling sage hurt them.

3. When these two do not injuriously affect each other, their good influences converge in the virtue of the Tao.

CHAPTER 61. 1. What makes a great state is its being like a low-lying, down-flowing stream; it becomes the centre to which tend all the small States under Heaven.

2. To illustrate from the case of all females: the female always overcomes the male by her stillness. Stillness may be considered a sort of abasement.

3. Thus it is that a great state, by condescending to small states, gains them for itself; and that small states, by abasing themselves to a great state, win it over to them. In the one case the abasement leads to gaining adherents, in the other case to procuring favour.

4. The great state only wishes to unite men together and nourish them; a small state only wishes to be received by, and to serve, the other. Each gets what it desires, but the great state must learn to abase itself.

CHAPTER 62. 1.
Tao has of all things the most honoured place.
No treasures give good men so rich a grace;
Bad men it guards, and doth their ill efface.

2. Its admirable words can purchase honour; its admirable deeds can raise their performer above others. Even men who are not good are not abandoned by it.

3. Therefore when the sovereign occupies his place as the son of Heaven, and he has appointed his three ducal ministers, though a prince were to send in a round symbol-of-rank large enough to fill both the hands, and that as the precursor of the team of horses in the court-yard, such an offering would not be equal to a lesson of this Tao, which one might present on his knees.

4. Why was it that the ancients prized this Tao so much? Was it not because it could be got by seeking for it, and the guilty could escape from the stain of their guilt by it? This is the reason why all under Heaven consider it the most valuable thing.

CHAPTER 63. 1. It is the way of the Tao to act without thinking of acting; to conduct affairs without feeling the trouble of them; to taste without discerning any flavour; to consider what is small as great, and a few as many; and to recompense injury with kindness.

2. The master of it anticipates things that are difficult while they are easy, and does things that would become great while they are small. All difficult things in the world are sure to arise from a previous state in which they were easy, and all great things from one in which they were small. Therefore the sage, while he never does what is great, is able on that account to accomplish the greatest things.

3. He who lightly promises is sure to keep but little faith; he who is continually thinking things easy is sure to find them difficult. Therefore the sage sees difficulty even in what seems easy, and so never has any difficulties.

CHAPTER 64. 1. That which is at rest is easily kept hold of; before a thing has given indications of its presence, it is easy to take measures against it; that which is brittle is easily broken; that which is very small is easily dispersed. Action should be taken before a thing has made its appearance; order should be secured before disorder has begun.

2. The tree which fills the arms grew from the tiniest sprout; the tower of nine storeys rose from a small heap of earth; the journey of a thousand li commenced with a single step.

3. He who acts with an ulterior purpose does harm; he who takes hold of a thing in the same way loses his hold. The sage does not act so, and therefore does no harm; he does not lay hold so, and therefore does not lose his hold. But people in their conduct of affairs are constantly ruining them when they are on the eve of success. If they were careful at the end, as they should be at the beginning, they would not so ruin them.

4. Therefore the sage desires what other men do not desire, and does not prize things difficult to get; he learns what other men do

not learn, and turns back to what the multitude of men have passed by. Thus he helps the natural development of all things, and does not dare to act with an ulterior purpose of his own.

CHAPTER 65. 1. The ancients who showed their skill in practising the Tao did so not to enlighten the people, but rather to make them simple and ignorant.

2. The difficulty in governing the people arises from their having much knowledge. He who tries to govern a state by his wisdom is a scourge to it; while he who does not try to do so is a blessing.

3. He who knows these two things finds in them also his model and rule. Ability to know this model and rule constitutes what we call the mysterious excellence of a governor. Deep and far-reaching is such mysterious excellence, showing indeed its possessor as opposite to others, but leading them to a great conformity to him.

CHAPTER 66. 1. That whereby the rivers and seas are able to receive the homage and tribute of all the valley streams, is their skill in being lower than they—it is thus that they are the kings of them all. So it is that the sage ruler, wishing to be above men, puts himself by his words below them, and, wishing to be before them, places his person behind them.

2. In this way though he has his place above them, men do not feel his weight, nor though he has his place before them, do they feel it an injury to them.

3. Therefore all in the world delight to exalt him and do not weary of him. Because he does not strive, no one finds it possible to strive with him.

CHAPTER 67. 1. All the world says that, while my Tao is great, it yet appears to be inferior to other systems of teaching. Now it is just its greatness that makes it seem to be inferior. If it were like any other system, for long would its smallness have been known!

2. But I have three precious things which I prize and hold fast. The first is gentleness; the second is economy; and the third is shrinking from taking precedence of others.

3. With that gentleness I can be bold; with that economy I can be liberal; shrinking from taking precedence of others, I can become a vessel of the highest honour. Nowadays they give up gentleness and are all for being bold; economy, and are all for being liberal; the hindmost place, and seek only to be foremost—of all which the end is death.

4. Gentleness is sure to be victorious even in battle, and firmly to maintain its ground. Heaven will save its possessor, by his very gentleness protecting him.

CHAPTER 68. He who in Tao's wars has skill
    Assumes no martial port;
  He who fights with most good will
    To rage makes no resort.
  He who vanquishes yet still
    Keeps from his foes apart;
  He whose hests men most fulfil
    Yet humbly plies his art.
Thus we say, "He ne'er contends,
    And therein is his might."
Thus we say, "Men's wills he bends,
    That they with him unite."

Thus we say, "Like Heaven's his ends,
    No sage of old more bright."

CHAPTER 69. 1. A master of the art of war has said, "I do not dare to be the host to commence the war; I prefer to be the guest to act on the defensive. I do not dare to advance an inch; I prefer to retire a foot." This is called marshalling the ranks where there are no ranks; baring the arms to fight where there are no arms to bare; grasping the weapon where there is no weapon to grasp; advancing against the enemy where there is no enemy.

2. There is no calamity greater than lightly engaging in war. To do that is near losing the gentleness which is so precious. Thus it is that when opposing weapons are actually crossed, he who deplores the situation conquers.

CHAPTER 70. 1. My words are very easy to know, and very easy to practise; but there is no one in the world who is able to know and able to practise them.

2. There is an originating and all-comprehending principle in my words, and an authoritative law for the things which I enforce. It is because they do not know these that men do not know me.

3. They who know me are few, and I am on that account the more to be prized. It is thus that the sage wears a poor garb of hair cloth, while he carries his signet of jade in his bosom.

CHAPTER 71. 1. To know and yet think we do not know is the highest attainment; not to know and yet think we do know is a disease.

2. It is simply by being pained at the thought of having this disease that we are preserved from it. The sage has not the disease. He knows the pain that would be inseparable from it, and therefore he does not have it.

CHAPTER 72. 1. When the people do not fear what they ought to fear, that which is their great dread will come on them.

2. Let them not thoughtlessly indulge themselves in their ordinary life; let them not act as if weary of what that life depends on.

3. It is by avoiding such indulgence that such weariness does not arise.

4. Therefore the sage knows these things of himself, but does not parade his knowledge; loves, but does not appear to set a value on, himself. And thus he puts the latter alternative away and makes choice of the former.

CHAPTER 73. 1. He whose boldness appears in his daring to do wrong, in defiance of the laws is put to death; he whose boldness appears in his not daring to do so lives on. Of these two cases the one appears to be advantageous, and the other to be injurious. But

> When Heaven's anger smites a man,
> Who the cause shall truly scan?

On this account the sage feels a difficulty as to what to do in the former case.

2. It is the Way of Heaven not to strive, and yet it skilfully overcomes; not to speak, and yet it is skilful in obtaining a reply; does not call, and yet men come to it of themselves. Its demonstrations are quiet, and yet its plans are skilful and effective.

The meshes of the net of Heaven are large; far apart, but letting nothing escape.

CHAPTER 74. 1. The people do not fear death; to what purpose is it to try to frighten them with death? If the people were always in awe of death, and I could always seize those who do wrong and put them to death, who would dare to do wrong?

2. There is always One who presides over the infliction death. He who would inflict death in the room of him who so presides over it may be described as hewing wood instead of a great carpenter. Seldom is it that he who undertakes the hewing, instead of the great carpenter, does not cut his own hands!

CHAPTER 75. 1. The people suffer from famine because of the multitude of taxes consumed by their superiors. It is through this that they suffer famine.

2. The people are difficult to govern because of the excessive agency of their superiors in governing them. It is through this that they are difficult to govern.

3. The people make light of dying because of the greatness of their labours in seeking for the means of living. It is this which makes them think light of dying. Thus it is that to leave the subject of living altogether out of view is better than to set a high value on it.

CHAPTER 76. 1. Man at his birth is supple and weak; at his death, firm and strong. So it is with all things. Trees and plants, in their early growth, are soft and brittle; at their death, dry and withered.

2. Thus it is that firmness and strength are the concomitants of death; softness and weakness, the concomitants of life.

3. Hence he who relies on the strength of his forces does not conquer; and a tree which is strong will fill the outstretched arms, and thereby invites the feller.

4. Therefore the place of what is firm and strong is below, and that of what is soft and weak is above.

CHAPTER 77. 1. May not the Way or Tao of Heaven be compared to the method of bending a bow? The part of the bow which was high is brought low, and what was low is raised up. So Heaven diminishes where there is superabundance, and supplements where there is deficiency.

2. It is the Way of Heaven to diminish superabundance, and to supplement deficiency. It is not so with the way of man. He takes away from those who have not enough to add to his own superabundance.

3. Who can take his own superabundance and therewith serve all under Heaven? Only he who is in possession of the Tao!

4. Therefore the ruling sage acts without claiming the results as his; he achieves his merit and does not rest arrogantly in it: he does not wish to display his superiority.

CHAPTER 78. 1. There is nothing in the world more soft and weak than water, and yet for attacking things that are firm and strong there is nothing that can take precedence of it—for there is nothing so effectual for which it can be changed.

2. Everyone in the world knows that the soft overcomes the hard, and the weak the strong, but no one is able to carry it out in practice.

3. Therefore a sage has said,

"He who accepts his State's reproach,
    Is hailed therefore its altars' lord;
To him who bears men's direful woes
    They all the name of King accord."

4. Words that are strictly true seem to be paradoxical.

CHAPTER 79. 1. When a reconciliation is effected between two parties after a great animosity, there is sure to be a grudge remaining in the mind of the one who was wrong. And how can this be beneficial to the other?

2. Therefore to guard against this, the sage keeps the left-hand portion of the record of the engagement, and does not insist on the speedy fulfilment of it by the other party. So, he who has the attributes of the Tao regards only the conditions of the engagement, while he who has not those attributes regards only the conditions favourable to himself.

3. In the Way of Heaven, there is no partiality of love; it is always on the side of the good man.

CHAPTER 80. 1. In a little state with a small population, I would so order it that, though there were individuals with the abilities of ten or a hundred men, there should be no employment of them; I would make the people, while looking on death as a grievous thing, yet not remove elsewhere to avoid it.

2. Though they had boats and carriages, they should have no occasion to ride in them; though they had buff coats and sharp weapons, they should have no occasion to don or use them.

3. I would make the people return to the use of knotted cords instead of the written characters.

4. They should think their coarse food sweet; their plain clothes beautiful; their poor dwellings places of rest; and their common simple ways sources of enjoyment.

5. There should be a neighbouring state within sight, and the voices of the fowls and dogs should be heard all the way from it to us, but I would make the people to old age, even to death, not have any intercourse with it.

CHAPTER 81. 1. Sincere words are not fine; fine words are not sincere. Those who are skilled in the Tao do not dispute about it; the disputatious are not skilled in it. Those who know the Tao are not extensively learned; the extensively learned do not know it.

2. The sage does not accumulate for himself. The more that he expends for others, the more does he possess of his own; the more that he gives to others, the more does he have himself.

3. With all the sharpness of the Way of Heaven, it injures not; with all the doing in the way of the sage he does not strive.